9 Life Altering Lessons:

Secrets of the
Mystery Schools Unveiled

By: Kala Ambrose

9 Life Altering Lessons: Secrets of the Mystery Schools Unveiled
Copyright© 2007 by Reality Press
All rights reserved.

Reality Press
An imprint of Reality Entertainment, Inc.

For information contact:

REALITY ENTERTAINMENT
P.O. Box 91
Foresthill, CA 95631

ph: 530-367-5389, fx: 530-367-3024

www.reality-entertainment.com

ISBN: 978-1-934588-03-1
Printed in the United States of America

Introduction

Long before the civilizations of Lemuria or Atlantis, Mystery Schools existed, sharing their wisdom and light on Earth. To answer the question, what is a mystery school, would be similar to attempting to explain the nature of humanity, as they are intertwined together. The schools are always working in some form of service to humanity, both in the seen and the unseen. As humanity evolves, the teachings continue to advance offering their wisdom for those who are ready to enter the temple and become a student of the esoteric teachings.

Some of the more well-known schools were in Sumeria, India, Egypt, Greece, and Celtic Europe, though there were many other esoteric schools around the world and certainly being one of the best known, does not imply being the best. Legends, fables and stories regarding the esoteric teachings and mystery schools have spread over into secret societies and branched out into other groups and organizations. It is not the focus of this book to teach the history of the mystery schools in the east and west, nor is it an attempt to explain all of the details involved, for this material can be found recorded elsewhere.

The purpose of this book is to invite you to pull up a chair and join us here for a thought-provoking conversation, like philosophers have done throughout the ages. I've spent this lifetime and others engaged in conversations such as these. Some call me a teacher. I like to say I do not teach, rather I help souls remember who they are. This knowledge is timeless and universal and belongs to no one and everyone all at the same time. Each person retains this information deep within their soul where they hold the key. When they are ready to release this wisdom and remember who they are and why they are here, they do so. For some people, the way to take this journey is through the mystery schools with a teacher and a guide. If I may be of some service in this capacity along their journey, I am pleased to do so.

During the time we share here together, my wish is that this book will stir your soul, entertain your thoughts and inspire you to explore the magnificence of who you are. Have no doubt that you are a most unique and beautiful soul and have much to give and share here and now in this beautiful universe and earth on which we reside.

It is not possible to fully discourse or teach these nine lessons here in this book, for the extent of their depth and wisdom would take volumes. It is also difficult to create a bibliography of sources as the resources provided in this book have been shared in private mystery schools in oral fashion for thousands of years. However, the information provided here will most definitely help one decide if they would like to study the esoteric teachings further and learn more.

I'd like to dedicate this book to Tim, whose steadfast love and encouragement cradles and nurtures me, while inspiring me to let my spirit soar and to Brandon, whose soul and very essence reminds me everyday of how incredibly beautiful and pure we all are.

I'd also like to thank Warren and Laura Croyle, John Jay Harper and Philip Gardiner, who remind me that angels walk this earth and live here amongst us, giving, sharing and loving in many ways.

Thank you also to the many beings and souls of light, my spiritual teachers on this plane and many others, who give, guide and encourage so lovingly with me on every step of my journey, my heart with yours.

My love and appreciation goes out to the esoteric students who study with me at the school of Stella Maris. Their dedication and love creates a beautiful light in the world and it is a joy to share this time with them.

And to you Dear Reader, thank you for allowing us to share this moment together. Your light shines brightly and there is no one like you. You have a great purpose and meaning for being here, right now, at this time and I honor you, soul to soul.

Enjoy the Journey,

Kala

Table of Contents

Chapter One

Everything Old is New "Age" Again

*"Never regard study as a duty, but as an enviable opportunity to learn
to know the liberating influence of beauty in the realm of the spirit
for your own personal joy and to the profit of the community
to which your later works belong."*
-- Albert Einstein --

Hello, my name is Kala.

I'm not here to teach you anything; rather I'm here to help you remember
what you already know at a soul level. I teach at the school of Stella Maris,
what are called esoteric teachings, which are also referred to as wisdom teachings, enlightenment teachings and mystery school teachings.

These teachings have been shared orally from teacher to student, through
the ages of humanity. Some of the most recognized are the teachings from
ancient Egypt, Greece and Celtic Europe, and others are from the ancient
wisdom of Sumeria and India. These esoteric teachings are much older than
this earth and the wisdom they offer is of most benefit when one discovers
or rather uncovers, what is unseen rather than seen.   On some occasions,
sacred parts of the material presented are written and recorded, as is found in
symbols, scrolls and inscribed stones and parchments, which are occasionally
discovered around the world. The teachings come from the other planes of
existence. They are introduced to the mind and then experienced through the
heart and soul. Perhaps it could be more accurately described to say that they
are absorbed within to gain new life, rather than being committed only to

memory. It has been the position of mystery schools to teach students in this manner and has been found to be the most effective.

These teachings can not be completely experienced or mastered by reading a book or taking a workshop. They are designed to serve as guides along your journey of self-exploration and path to enlightenment. They have a way of touching your heart and soul, leading the mind in many different directions, while stirring the emotions. Most importantly, even when one reads and discusses just one of these lessons, they discover layers upon layers in each teaching and none of them can be absorbed in one sitting.

When working with beginning students, the goal of a mystery school teacher is to present a brief exposure to some of the concepts of the wisdom teachings. The teacher can be viewed as a gardener, planting seeds of knowledge in the mind of the burgeoning student. The hope is that the student contemplates and cultivates these thoughts so that the seeds will grow and yield fruit in the future.

As with any garden, it takes the dedicated effort of working with light, earth, elements and energy to produce a garden with delightful results and abundant yields. This is how the teachings grow, rather than you absorbing them, they take root and absorb into you, forever changing who you are and how you view the world. Rather than you controlling the garden, you become the garden. Think on this, for you are about to begin a journey into the esoteric teachings. With each lesson that unfolds, the mysteries deepen and intertwine. Are you ready?

Let's begin....

If you have proceeded this far and have decided to take the journey offered in this book, you are stepping into a world referred to in the mystery schools as becoming a Neophyte. Let's take a moment here and explain to you a few of the terms which are used in the mystery schools. A new student to the school is described as a Neophyte. The definition of a Neophyte according to

Webster's dictionary is a beginner or novice, to bring forth, newly planted. This is pretty straight-forward. In the esoteric definition, a Neophyte is a student who has just become aware that they may be more than what they previously considered themselves to be. They understand that what they thought to be their consciousness may only be a small part of what lies beneath the surface of their thoughts and emotions. For many students, a life-altering experience or intense soul searching has prompted them to look for answers and their journey has led them to the ancient mystery teachings. They may have connected with their intuition bringing them to a variety of new and sometimes unexplained experiences. Many find that working with an esoteric teacher, enhances their journey and serves as a guide to help remember what they already know on a core soul level.

A student who enters the school remains a Neophyte until they progress to the next level, which is called an Initiate. The definition of an Initiate according to dictionary.com is to admit or accept with formal rites into an organization or group, secret knowledge or adult society.

Each mystery school has their guidelines for what a Neophyte must first learn and accomplish before they can proceed to becoming an Initiate. The ancient schools had very demanding protocols for what a person must excel in and learn regarding the esoteric teachings, before they could proceed further into the mysteries. This was for the protection of the student and for the school. This is why a series of checkpoints are set in the schools, both on the Earth plane and on the other spiritual planes. In most situations, the student knows when they are truly ready to progress. Typically it is after a series of rituals and experiences have been entered into and successfully transcended, through extensive work training and journeys on the other planes.

Perhaps one of the most misunderstood definitions has been the use of the word esoteric. The word esoteric, according to dictionary.com, means: understood by or meant for only the select few who have special knowledge or interests. This definition is often taken out of context. The teachings are available for anyone with an open mind and heart who is also committed to putting the time, energy and effort into doing the inner work necessary to look deep within their heart, mind and soul.

The reason that esoteric teachings are taught to so few, is that when most people are introduced to the teachings and begin to understand the great amount of introspection involved in the study of these teachings, most are not interested in taking this journey. For various reasons, it is not the right time for them to look inward to see why they act, think and feel the way the do, as well as explore the other inner thoughts they must ponder.

Also contrary to popular belief, one does not join a mystery school and then is handed a secret book with all of the sacred knowledge of the world. Even if such a book could be written, the answers are so complex, and also amazingly simple at the same time, that the person reading them would not even understand the book if it lay right before them. This is because there are a series of sacred passages which were created, long ago which rest inside each person. These passages have portals of entry into the heart, mind and soul which are not opened until chemical and alchemical changes inside the body and mind are secreted. When this magical act occurs, these gates swing open fully and the wisdom is granted to the student. We'll speak more on these changes in the coming chapters.

There are no shortcuts to creating this effect. It is a process which each person goes through, following the teachings along the path, solving clues and ancient mysteries, all the while opening further through experiences and evolving at each step until the mysteries are released from the inside out. As Above, So Below, As Within, So Without. Think on these teachings, they will come to mean more to you; the longer you study them.

Mystery school teachers prefer that you do not change any belief that you currently have as you begin to study with them. They are not a religion and they are seen as an accompaniment to any religious or spiritual beliefs you currently have. They also state, as I tell every student whom I teach from day one, "Do not believe a word I say, all that is asked of you, is that you listen with an open mind and consider what is being presented. If it resonates with you, then take it and think further upon it, if it does not, we only ask that you do not disregard it completely, but rather file this information away to reconsider at another point and time. There is no judgment, only acknowledgement and acceptance. I state this for two very important reasons, the first being that this journey is about self-exploration and discovery; not listening blindly to another to find out how to live one's life. Second, is that it is very important for each student to learn to discern within themselves what feels right for them. As students of the wisdom teachings, they are taught to go within and trust the wisdom coming from their heart, rather than what another person may tell them is the right information.

We must also delve into the definition of what is a mystery school? Mystery schools are often referred to as temples, and there have been and continue to be physical temples and centers built in locations around the world. Mystery schools are also inner temples which are created within the heart, mind and soul as well as in the other planes. Depending upon their location, some schools choose to have physical temples for all who are interested to attend lectures and public events for educational purposes. At the same time, some of the actual deeper lessons are held in sacred places in nature, where students connect with the natural forces of the ocean, or amongst the trees or deep within the mountains and caves for certain rituals and powerful introspective experiences.

A student who is willing to step into the study of the mysteries, will soon discover that how they feel about nature and the world around them alters and grows in depth. In addition, along with this discovery, they begin to see that there are other like-minded individuals like themselves who are joined in the pursuit of wisdom, compassion and service. Their chance meetings of these people increase significantly and in synchronistic patterns as they progress.

The last definition before we proceed further is the explanation of what is known as "The Brotherhood." To define the Brotherhood, goes much deeper than a textbook explanation. To summarize briefly, the Brotherhood is a group of Ascended Masters who exist in a spiritual hierarchy on the other planes. These souls, male and female, work together in service to help humanity advance further along the path and advance into each age. As students progress, they first meet their spirit guides on the other side who assist them with their learning. Students who progress further, eventually work with the Brotherhood, oft times in dream states and in meditation and other ways, both on the earth plane and the spiritual planes.

During dream state experiences, which I refer to my students as attending "Night School," guides and other light beings approach the student and begin to work with them in this state. One could view the Brotherhood as a university in the other dimensions, who's mission is to educate, inspire and serve, in love for all of humanity. Many of these advanced beings are souls who once walked the earth and are considered to be master teachers including Jesus, Buddha, Mary/Isis, Kwan Yin, Confucius, Krishna and many others.

Without going too deep into this teaching, which is taught to all mystery school students, we will say briefly that the Brotherhood works with many here on the earth plane. Just as there are chakras within the body, there are also chakra points on the earth and some of these sacred places are areas in which the Brotherhood likes to frequent and conduct spiritual work while on this plane.

It should be said however, that in the esoteric/wisdom teachings, we teach that all of the Earth is sacred and everywhere is sacred ground and should be respected as such. In addition, when one is in communication with the Brotherhood, this connection can be accessed anywhere in the world, one does not need to travel to a certain location. What is worthy of note however, is that each person will find that they are drawn to or connected to certain elements and spaces on the Earth. Those areas serve to help open and activate energies and portals within themselves, which further enhance the experience and communication with the Brotherhood and other advanced beings.

Individuals and groups who work with the Brotherhood have journeyed through the esoteric/wisdom teachings, in one form or another, and wish to be in service to humanity. They are often misunderstand as people who are willing to make great sacrifices, but it never feels like a sacrifice to the person as they experience great joy and fulfillment in the work that they do. They serve in many ways including inspiring and teaching, giving freely of time and energy to others, and working to send love and light to the earth and all of humanity. There are many people on the earth doing this type of service, and one does not need to be part of a mystery school to connect in this manner. Many souls have spent many lifetimes in mystery schools and other teachings and have come back in this lifetime to be of direct service in the best way possible as it is shown to them. This is one of the precepts of our school, Stella Maris, where we say, "Many Paths, One Destination." There are many paths one can walk to gain experience and wisdom and reconnect with their soul's purpose for being here in this lifetime. Stella Maris and many other wisdom schools are just one option among many wonderful doorways on the path.

Throughout this book, hidden meanings are layered throughout the chapters, in what are known as "pearls of wisdom" in the teachings. The esoteric teachings are often referred to as a process of peeling back the onion, implying that they have many layers. As you read and contemplate and perhaps re-read a section again, you'll find that new ideas and concepts enter your mind. This is the way things are done and so the best way to begin is to understand that we are all on a journey and that knowing the answers is not as important as the process of how we get there.

Perhaps this sounds more confusing than when we first started, but that is the way of the esoteric teachings. At their best, they stir the mind, lift the heart and stimulate the soul. The rest of this book will begin to explain what we describe as Nine Life-Altering Lessons. They are ancient lessons, which are being described now in current expressions as we move into this Age of Aquarius. It is a most exciting time to be alive and here on the earth plane, for we are ushering in a time which has not been experienced before in this way. Each person here on this earth, has a part to play in this progression. It is no surprise that so many are awakening to their divine purpose, longing to understand what it is they are here to do during this lifetime. It is my hope that this book will help you to discover, discern and ponder many questions about yourself including, "Who Am I" and "Why Am I Here."

It is also my wish that this book will stimulate your mind into delving deeper into the insightful mysteries of the teachings and encourages you to travel further into the esoteric knowledge of yourself and your soul. In short, I am saying, as the ancient Greek Temples inscribed above their archways… "Man, Know Thyself."

Remember, I can not teach you anything, I can only help you to remember who you are.

A tiny but powerful candle light has appeared before you, shall we continue together on this journey?

Chapter Two

Lesson One:
We Live In A Magical Universe

"The important thing is not to stop questioning.
Curiosity has its own reason for existing.
One can not help but be in awe when he contemplates
the mysteries of eternity, of life, of the marvelous structure of reality.
It is enough if one tries merely to comprehend a little of this mystery every day.
Never lose a holy curiosity."
-- Albert Einstein --

The cyclical nature of the universe has been understood by the mystery schools since their inception. Man over time, has become confused, believing that Time is linear and proceeding in a straight line. Yet, ask any history scholar who researches time-lines for a living and they will admit that history does in fact repeat itself, repeatedly! And with this repetition, humanity appears to make the same mistakes, encounter the same experiences and relive commonalities over and over again.

Why is this? The answer is that we are here on this earth plane to learn and grow and how we achieve this is by encountering experiences (lessons) which we repeat over and over until we understand what we need to learn from this experience. Once the point or points of the experience have been understood, the lesson no longer needs to be repeated and we continue on to a more complicated lesson. This takes the knowledge we have gained and continues on to a deeper lesson on our path to wisdom and enlightenment. Think of this concept much as one would when studying principles of mathematics. At first, we are introduced to the concepts and are instructed in the ways of addition and subtraction. Once you have achieved mastery over this, you move forward to multiplication and division, which are more complex forms of the same ideal. The same would occur with Algebra and Geometry.

The ancients taught about the cyclical nature of our world, and our existence using simple and complex examples to get their points across. They taught the cycles of change describing the seasons as they repeated each year. In more esoteric lessons, they taught about the Ouroboros, the symbol of a serpent swallowing its tail. Both were meant to teach that we are always in the process of creating and recreating and this fluctuates with our active/solar side and our passive/lunar side. It is the balance of all things and the understanding that they are not separate, but rather part of the whole and both are required for the full completion of the experience. For example, which living creature would you say is more important, a Cow or a Bee? Are you sure? Do both not have something to provide to this world? If we examine these two closely, we see the Cow, gentle, passive, giving, in deep thought and when we look at the Bee, we see activity, creation, moving from one experience to the next, sharing as it travels. Do not both of these natures exist in us as well? At times, we must be contemplative in our surroundings, and at other times, we must take action and create to nourish not only ourselves, but others. When we are out of balance, we are too far in one of these directions. If we stay active all of the time, there is no time for inner contemplation and self discovery. In this state, we are unable to digest what we have experienced. In the same way, if we are too still and just spend time in thought, we miss the opportunities provided for us to grow and expand our consciousness. The first key to learning as a Neophyte is to understand that we must work to achieve balance in both sectors. This has been taught in Eastern cultures using the symbol of the Yin/Yang, which explains that both are required to make the whole. Neither is better or right, both are equally important. We must have passive time to reflect and active time to grow and we must face our shadow selves in order to fully see the light.

This understanding has been taught, not only in the mystery teachings, but also by Plato, who described the universe as a circular immortal being. This cyclical teaching is also described in indigenous tribe's teachings, Celtic and Norse teachings, Chinese and other Asian teachings, Egyptian teachings,

Alchemist teachings, and Aztec, Greek, Gnostic, and Hindu teachings. In modern times, psychologists including Carl Jung also wrote about the Ouroboros, describing it as an archetype with great significance to understanding the human psyche.

You will soon discover here dear student, that in the first approach with each lesson one only experiences the outer layer. As your consciousness opens and expands, you will find deeper meaning and truth in each one. As we have said, many esoteric teachers refer to this as peeling back the layers of the onion. Have you ever peeled an onion? There is layer after layer to be pulled and this analogy is helpful in understanding the delicate layers that exist together to make the whole, in both the teachings and the understanding of the cosmos and the universe.

At this point in the teachings, the Neophyte student begins to delve further into this lesson by breaking down these concepts and thinking of them on a scale we all experience on the earth plane. These are the four seasons of Fall, Winter, Spring and Summer which are marked by the Equinox's and Solstice's. These markers of time have been celebrated in one form or another by almost every culture on earth, past and present. When one studies with a mystery school, the deeper meanings of the equinox's and solstices are revealed, including what energies are present during these times and how one can embrace this energy and connect through rituals and meditative experiences. Many wonderful books discuss in great detail the meanings of the equinox's and solstice's, so we will not attempt to explain the full meaning of these seasonal events here at this time.

It has been rumored that in the ancient mystery schools of Egypt, the Initiate was taught through a series of teachings which are similarly represented in the Higher Arcana Tarot cards. The student would enter as "The Fool," meaning at that time, unaware of the greater consciousness and the deeper mysteries. Many people cringe at the word "fool" as modern connotations with it would describe making an embarrassment of oneself, or appearing foolish. However, the deeper meaning of this card is much different. To embrace the esoteric journey, one has to be willing to admit that they may not know all the answers as they may have previously thought and they must be willing to take a leap of faith into the unknown. The Fool begins their journey, with no idea of what is in store for their future or what experiences await them. They bring an open mind and heart to begin their journey, and are willing to take risks and confront their fears. The number of the fool card interestingly, is zero, again creating that perfect circle. All things are cyclical.

The Higher Arcana of the tarot cards are as follows: The Fool, The Magician, The High Priestess, The Empress, The Emperor, The Hierophant, The Lovers, The Chariot, Strength, The Hermit, Wheel of Fortune, Justice, The Hanged Man, Death, Temperance, The Tower, The Star, The Moon, The Sun, Judgment and The World. Throughout this book, esoteric (hidden) references to the meanings of these cards will be shared including how they correspond with many of the teachings. Understanding the tarot will have tremendous value to you on your path as an esoteric student and can serve as a wonderful guide along your journey, once you have developed good discernment, a topic which will be discussed further in another chapter. Some students believe that if they understand the tarot, then they also understand the mystery teachings, however, this is not the case. However, studying the tarot and connecting with it, opens up the mind and gives valuable clues as you proceed on your journey from Neophyte to Initiate. In some tarot decks, there are wonderful, educational symbols hidden in the decks for the student to uncover. Once having mastered and understood the tarot, the student receives guidance and helpful clues as to what experiences await them as they proceed on this path to realization and enlightenment.

This is all well and good, but the question arises, how does this teach us about the universe being magical? To elaborate, once we understand that everything repeats itself, we can begin to remove ourselves from this cycle, also known as the wheel of fortune or wheel of karma. The primary basis of this teaching is that when you remove yourself from the wheel of karma, you also free your mind from existing in only the lower levels of thought and energy and begin to connect with the higher levels of existence which are open to all who seek.

In the teachings to the Neophytes, it is said: When a student first glimpses this truth and the thought of it begins to burn in their mind, that more can exist beyond what they first thought possible, the first glimpse of light dawns on the horizon for them and they decide at that moment to begin their quest. They soon realize that if they can become the master of their thoughts and emotions, they can remove themselves from this cycle of the wheel of karma and grow closer to experiencing their true inner selves.

Once the student steps outside of the belief that their previous basic thoughts are the only thoughts which exist in life, they open up the floodgates to the greater possibilities the universe has to offer. This is where true magic begins!

The first lesson given to the Neophyte is:

We Live In A Magical Universe,

which means that,

The Possibilities Of What We Can Create Are Infinite!

This does not mean we do not have to work hard to achieve this ability of creation or that universal laws are not put into place for our protection. Imagine, if this was not so! Many a Neophyte student will complain when first taught this lesson, saying, "Well if this is true, then how come when I think hard about wanting this or that, nothing happens?" The first concept to understand is that protective measures have been put into place by the universe to protect you from greater harm until you mature to a level to take it on for yourself, much as a parent does for a child.

Imagine if you will, if you could just have a thought and it would occur instantly. What if it was truly that easy, that whatever you think, would manifest instantly before your very eyes. Sound good? Ok, then put down this book, and take a minute. Close your eyes and think about every thought you have had in this past week, remember to include all of the positive thoughts and all of the negative thoughts. What have you created this past week? Are you pleased with these creations, the thoughts you have had about yourself, your family, friends, co-workers and even strangers. When watching a sporting event, do you really mean what you say when you chant that you wish for the other team to literally be crushed? When yelling at a stranger in the car in front of you on the freeway, is that really how you would like that person to spend the remainder of their days on this earth? In frustration with your spouse or children, would you really like it if your thoughts became reality? What about the thoughts you've had about yourself, even looking into the mirror one day, would you like those thoughts that you've had about yourself during that time to magnify as you thought them to be?

For most of you reading this book, the answers to these questions would be No; you don't really want those things to happen, when you really think about the consequences they would bring. This is why these measures were put into place, so that until each of us did the work to unlock the codes inside of us where we can activate our thoughts into reality, we can not actively create on the whims of our random emotions and thoughts. It is fortunate in many ways, that most people have such a short attention span and quickly move on to other random thoughts with little energy attached to any of them!

In the next chapter, we will discuss why it is so important to master our thoughts and emotions before we begin to actively and consciously create. We are subconsciously creating all the time, whether we realize it or not, which delves into the teachings of the law of attraction. What we think, manifests itself into our lives. However conscious creation is even stronger and thusly safeguards were put into place for this magic as well.

Be that as it may, we do live in a magical universe, which listens to every thought we have, every word we say and every action we take and it responds accordingly, like a genie following our commands. Therefore, a Neophyte student must understand this most important universal law of thought and attraction. For it can be the most exhilarating, awe-inspiring and possibly terrifying realization, once one understands the depth of where our thoughts and emotions can take us in a moment's notice.

There is a point of retreat which I offer to my Neophyte students when they first begin the Esoteric Classes. They are invited to attend three beginner's classes, in which I explain the basic tenets of these concepts. At the end of the third class, I invite them to cross the first line drawn in the sand as I describe it metaphorically.

Once they cross this line, this signifies that they have opened their minds to the first level of exploration and are ready to explore deeper into their consciousness. There is an old saying, "Ignorance is Bliss." What this means is that when one does not have knowledge of the teachings, one is blissfully unaware of what they are doing to create these actions in their life. This does not signify that one lives in bliss, but rather than one does not have the knowledge that; what one thinks, one creates in their life. Once a student has crossed this line in the sand of understanding and realizes this teaching, it is most difficult to turn back to the life they knew before, as they have the realization that can not be forgotten.

From there, the journey continues and there are many more lines to be crossed as the path of the esoteric student evolves. In the mystery teachings, one is taught that communication with the universe and the multi-verses travels faster than the speed of light; in fact it is instantaneous in many cases. As soon as you have the thought, you have already experienced it on some level, in some place, in some other time. Yes, esoteric teachers are aware that many scientists still agree with the theory of Einstein that communication does not travel faster than the speed of light, and I am not here to debate current scientific understanding. Science continues to evolve and expand its theories and good scientists are always open to new discoveries in their fields of research. I have the deepest respect for Einstein and his work and he remained open minded to understanding the world around us further and deeper, as evidenced in many of his quotes including:

"Reality is merely an illusion, albeit a very persistent one."

*"I maintain that cosmic religiousness is the strongest
and most noble driving force of scientific research."*

*"The most beautiful thing we can experience is the mysterious.
It is the source of all true art and all science.
He to whom this emotion is a stranger,
who can no longer pause to wonder and stand rapt in awe,
is as good as dead: his eyes are closed."*

and perhaps my favorite......

*"It would be possible to describe everything scientifically,
but it would make no sense; it would be without meaning,
as if you described a Beethoven symphony as a variation of wave pressure."*

Perhaps we can wonder, has Einstein already reincarnated back onto this planet and is currently at work pushing the boundaries of discovery into more scientific areas, including expounding upon his work and finding that some things do travel faster than the speed of light. This work has begun to be explored, as evidenced by a Paris research team in the 1980's which discovered that under certain conditions and circumstances, subatomic particles such as electrons are able to simultaneously communicate with each other. It was found that distance was not a factor in their ability to communicate, which revealed the understanding that the particles were aware of what the other particles were doing, regardless of how far away they were from each other. Fascinating isn't it? Mystics have taught a similar concept for eons, that We Are All One, and that as part of the Whole, the Energy/God/Spirit whatever you wish to call it, is always aware of you on some level. Esoteric teachers have always maintained, that when Science can work together with Spirituality, that greater understanding of both will be realized. Each side holds part of this knowledge. Working together, answers can be uncovered in the most profound life-altering discoveries.

If humanity could embrace and truly understand, that all things are connected and that what you do in thought, words and deeds affects not only you, but everyone and everything, imagine how we could change our world in a moment. All we would need is one moment of global consciousness and understanding and the world could be transformed. Perhaps we will see this occur in our future. However, in this moment, what we can do is continue to teach those who have eyes in which to see and ears in which to hear, to learn of the greater consciousness and the mysteries which are unveiled on the labyrinth path to wisdom.

When one begins to tackle this puzzle and peels back the first layer of the onion, the discovery is astounding. One begins to see that what appears to be real, is not and what appears to be illusion, is in fact real! Where does one go from here?

As this begins to sink in, your world is turned upside down. Everything you have been taught by society, by your families and your schools, you have just been told that it is not so, not as it appears. At first, you disbelieve and perhaps react with shock and return back to your "normal" life, thinking that this has all been a ridiculous discussion. However, for many of you, as the old saying goes, "When the Student is Ready, The Teacher Appears." You will find that rather than finding comfort in your old life, you now are left with a nagging feeling that you are close to discovering something within yourself which you've always felt deep inside. There is a part of you which calls out to you at night, or when you are alone in silent reflection, almost like a cry at times, wanting to be released and explored.

Perhaps something in this first lesson has touched you and now that it's been opened slightly, you find it hard to return to what you believed before. This part of you, from a soul level, is ready for more and won't give you peace. It is at this point, you make your first decision, which is whether you are ready to explore further or whether you will put these thoughts aside and go on as you have been before, until you feel ready to proceed further. This is one of the beautiful gifts of the Universe, as should this not be the right time for you,

you will have other opportunities to explore this if you so choose, in this lifetime and in others. Remember, the universe moves in a cyclical fashion, and it will come around again, Life indeed is just one big "Merry-Go-Round," which explains some of those déjà vu feelings you've had…

Once we begin to understand that the universe is indeed magical, the teachings proceed into the Initiate Level. The deeper secret teaching is:

When We Activate Our Consciousness,
We Become Magical Beings and Can Harness This Energy

When we activate our consciousness, the all seeing eye of the universe, then becomes aware of us and looks back at us! When we transform and become conscious creators, the energy transforms into an ocean of energy, rather than only previously receiving drops of water from the magical universe.

In that Moment of Awareness, Everything Changes.

To further explain … Universal energy flows continuously like a waterfall upon the earth plane. As our thoughts, words and deeds pour forth from each of us; they interact with this waterfall and are activated. Since they are created from the lower levels of our bodies, and are from our lower subconscious selves, the energy coming from them is from the emotional and mental bodies and is short lived. In this state, it interacts for a few brief moments of time with the waterfall, causing an action and reaction for us and then it is gone. Unless we hold on to this emotion or thought and keep sending it back to this waterfall, (which causes greater action and reaction to happen regarding this particular thought), it will dissipate quickly. Remember, it is the lower self sending out this energy from the emotional and mental bodies, which is tiring and exhaustive. The result is reactive only. Basically we send out a lower level desire or impulse and it is reflected back to us.

However, when we become "conscious creators," we are working from a higher level and from higher bodies within ourselves and we send out deliberate and focused energy to this universal waterfall. We are saying, "Now, I See You and You See Me." "I AM interacting with you and wish to magnify this energy with you to create an outcome." This of course, can be used for positive or negative effects. Some people choose not to follow the Path of Light and rather than work from their heart chakra, they prefer to conduct this from a lower level body to achieve the results they desire. This is short lived, as accessing energy at this level can be achieved, however, it has the detrimental effect of taking a harsh toll on the body and mind and eats away at all of the lower level bodies. This does not have the same effect when followed on the path of light course of action.

As the All Seeing Eye or Universal Energy becomes aware that you are "aware," its energy quickens and vibrates more excitedly with yours and things begin to happen at a faster pace. It has no problem keeping up with you, as quickly as you are willing to progress. At this point, you will just be beginning to see what truly is possible in such a magical universe. Indeed as we have said before, the possibilities are endless! However, it must be said, that at the Neophyte stage, one is better served to first master these nine teachings and understand both the concepts and the pitfalls before attempting to work with them. Otherwise consequences can result which are unwanted and the student may not be prepared to handle the resulting outcome. This is why esoteric teachers are so useful, both in past and present endeavors, to help guide the student through this process of reconnecting again. This book can only serve to stimulate your curiosity and perhaps begin or enhance your journey to explore these nine lessons.

To continue with this thought, think of Universal Energy as having the same effect as electricity. Electricity has great power. At first, in its raw unleashed form, it is exhilarating to see, as in a lightening storm. Should this storm approach closer to you and your home, you soon realize that it also has the power to cause great destruction. On the flip side, electricity when properly understood and harnessed can be used in whatever form you wish, including lighting and heating or cooling your home, along with many other wonderful forms of focused energy.

I trust dear student, that as you read this book, you are discovering that each mystery teaching contains a series of deeper and even more unique mysteries to unravel. The path of the Neophyte and the Esoteric Student is one of growth, understanding and evolvement. One must cultivate patience while at the same time, strive to remain open to new experiences, while questioning all experiences until discernment is found, which takes a significant amount of time. Rather than discouraging you from this path, my hope is that as these lessons unfold, that it stimulates your mind and stirs your soul, bringing forth long forgotten memories of who you used to be and who you are meant to be again... You have only to ask these questions to the universe, to begin your journey today.

As you read through the chapters, you will discover that each lesson builds from the previous one, methodically piecing together ancient mysteries. When you begin to solve these puzzles and connect the lessons together, you will find yourself becoming an Esoteric Student, preparing to journey into the ancient mysteries. The first step is to delve deeper into what is written here in this book, as there are hidden clues which you will uncover in time...

One of the teachings I share with my students, is the concept of spinning plates. Many students and some teachers believe that it takes an extraordinary amount of effort to access this energy. In the beginning, this is true for many people. However, one of the skills students develop over time is how to connect with the energy, creating the outcome they would like for it to achieve. Once you establish this connection, you need only to check in every so often to make sure it is still turning and twirling in a fashion which you would like for it to continue, recharging it with energy on an occasional basis so that it continues to move. You can see this when you observe a performer twirl plates on sticks. He begins by twirling one plate and then is able to go to the next and the next, until many plates are spinning. He only needs to touch each one gently to keep the momentum going on them. When he tires of the performance and it has lost its appeal, he simply pulls his attention from the plates, and does not give them any further energy, allowing them to come to an ending.

Think on this, where does your energy go, what do you pour your energy into on a daily basis? Are you satisfied with where your energy is going, what plates are spinning over your head right now…

If you have thought this over and these teachings interest and intrigue you, be prepared as you journey further, for the information may cause you to rethink and reconsider almost every aspect of your life.

Are You Ready To Walk This Path?

Chapter Three

Lesson Two:
We Are The Creation of Our Thoughts

"Mind is the Master power that molds and makes
And Man is Mind, and evermore he takes
The tool of Thought, and shaping what he wills,
Brings forth a thousand joys, a thousand ills:
He thinks in secret, and it comes to pass
Environment is but his looking glass."
-- James Allen --

Continuing on the mystery path, and the discussion regarding the wheel of karma, which we are attached to in our current existence, the question quickly arises, how do we remove ourselves from the wheel? The simplest way to teach or describe this lesson is to explain that every act, thought, deed, and word that we create, comes back to us through this wheel.

This is a difficult lesson for many students to embrace, for it is a major step in understanding that what you think, is not hidden, rather it is reflected all around you in your life. We have previously been taught that our thoughts were secret, that no one knew what we were thinking. What a profound concept, everything you think, is reflected and then created in your life. Once you begin to focus on this concept, that you create your reality, the awareness quickly sinks in that if you are displeased with any portion of your life, that according to this principle and universal law, you created and attracted these series of events into your life.

This concept forces the student to wrestle with the ego and the mind. We all want to believe that we are good people who do no harm to ourselves or others. To accept the idea that the negative events occurring in our lives are a direct reflection of our thoughts, words, actions and deeds is to embrace the fact that we can never blame another person again for anything that occurs in our lives. No one can ever again "make" us angry, we choose to be angry; no one can make us happy or sad, rather, we choose to have this emotion.

In addition, in some cases, we have brought this karma back with us from a previous incarnation and thusly have attracted these experiences to us again, in order to learn and master this lesson and move forward. When this is understood, it becomes pointless to keep up a wall in an attempt to avoid the experiences and difficulties of life, as they are being created or have been created by you to continue on your path of development. The quickest way to move through the lesson is with compassion and understanding for all involved, with the realization that this experience will soon pass, which allows the soul to be free to move on to new experiences. Many of these experiences quickly end when a student works through their fears, to the point where they are ready to see and speak their truth. For many, this is a most difficult task.

The Neophyte student is taught that if you do not like a certain aspect of your life, examine your thoughts and beliefs about this subject. To make a change in this area, begin by changing your thoughts. For example, many people say to justify their feelings or actions: "I can't help it, I was born this way or raised this way by my parents," or "You do not understand me, I am very sensitive." These are called defense mechanisms. To be a student of the esoteric teachings, you will need to embrace the understanding that heredity is a temporary situation, not a permanent one.

We are the creators of our destiny, and this occurs every moment of our lives. It is our decision as to whether it will be done consciously or unconsciously. When this is understood, one can no longer blame everyone and everything else for the situations surrounding them. As the student learns these concepts, they must take a deep look at their life and then begin to change the picture by an overhaul and reconstruction of their mind. This in turn, creates new chemical reactions in our bodies, moving from destructive chemicals created by worry, fear, stress and anxiety to love, peace, joy and abundance.

Another deeply surprising lesson is that, if you can think a thought, then it has already been experienced on some level. This teaching has been expressed by many inspired and creative people, including Walt Disney when he spoke, "If You Can Dream It, You Can Do It." The reason we do not create more with our minds is because the lower self and the ego is controlling. It prefers to stay with what is familiar, as the lower self deals with fear as a primary motivating factor. Ego works daily to convince the lower self and mind that this is the best choice. The mantra of the ego says, if one stays with the familiar, the fears have been weighed and considered and one will be in greater control of all situations. The belief is that in keeping with this system, one stays safe and prepared for whatever is going to happen next. The ego never lets the mind forget that a negative experience is always sure to be looming around the next corner. What the person does not see, is that the ego while doing this, slowly builds brick by brick, or shall we say, thought by thought, a wall around the person and the soul, which limits the person from the full expression of their soul. It also slows down one of the reasons to be on this plane, which is to gain and learn through experiences.

Do not feel badly if you find yourself in this situation, we all begin here as it is a natural reaction and the lower self is attempting to protect itself from further harm. This begins when we are young. We are the recipients of judgments and criticisms, which in turn induce a self-protective mechanism from within to build a wall of safety and defense. People quickly learn at a young age, that if they cry or appear weak to the masses of society, (which in esoteric teachings is often described as a herd mentality), they are only picked on further. The mind begins to agree with the reasoning of the ego, which rationalizes that if a wall is created, the person will appear indifferent and strong. With this armor in place, it will conceivably be easier to proceed further in life.

As an esoteric student however, the time has come to put down those walls, for while it is true that negative attacks no longer appear to affect you as deeply, it is also true that not much of anything can reach through to you, including love and positive energies. This wall quickly becomes a negative base of fear, full of judgmental and angry thoughts. One begins to realize that rather than keeping the world out, one instead has become a prisoner behind the wall. Esoterically, fear is the opposite of love and these are the two strongest emotions, which are polar opposites.

Many students do not understand the definition of fear and when asked, they will exclaim to me, "I am not a fearful person." I will then ask them, are you angry or judgmental? Do you experience feelings of greed or jealousy or have a sense that life is not fair, and that some people are undeserving of what they receive? Do you worry that you won't have enough? Are you uncomfortable being alone? Negative thinking in any nature, including living in delusion about situations and not dealing with things in life, are all part of fear. When faced with these questions, the student realizes that they do indeed live with some sort of fear.

Fear comes from lack of feeling love and it can be traced back through not feeling self-love. Until a person can truly love themselves, they can not be released from fear. Students at first do not understand this, they will challenge this teaching and say, "This is not true, I love my spouse, even though I do not truly love myself". Yet when discussion continues on this subject regarding the definition of higher forms of love, it becomes apparent they do not love unconditionally. Examples of loving unconditionally include: loving your spouse or partner regardless of their actions; giving your spouse or partner the freedom to experience life as they need to experience it without judgment or controlling thoughts; and loving your spouse or partner, even if they decide to no longer be with you and choose to go their own way. Bear in mind that loving unconditionally does not mean that you have to like or accept or live with the actions if they are too uncomfortable for you, it just means that you are able to maintain a higher form of unconditional love at the soul level. In its most simple form of understanding, it means that you can love the person at a soul level (higher self), but not necessarily their earthly (lower self) actions.

Before students can continue with the teachings of unconditional love, they must understand how the ego affects them in its current state of existence in the physical, emotional, mental and spiritual bodies.

Psychologists have debated for years about the ego and what effect it has on the personality. If this is a point of interest for you, there are many wonderful books which discuss psychology and the perspectives of the psychological understanding of ego and the mind. In this book, the philosophical discussion will be focused specifically on the effect of ego on the spiritual journey and with the soul. One of the books I recommend all students read to understand the power of thoughts and their effects on all of the bodies, is a very small and powerful book, *As A Man Thinketh*, which was written by James Allen almost a century ago.

To understand ego, is first to understand that as humans, we are not born with raging egos, (with the exception of a few souls who come back this way due to many lifetimes seeking power at any cost). For most people though, this is not the case. The ego develops, like all things in life, because it is fed. Most people are not aware how they feed their ego, because at the time, it appears they are just pursuing something which will lead to their eventual happiness.

In the teachings, we often use parables to explain how this occurs with ego. In this story, picture yourself as a young man. As a young man, you begin to desire something that you wish to have in your life, perhaps you wish to gain the attention and affection of a young girl. As you approach the young woman in an attempt to engage her in conversation, you are quickly rebuffed as she mentions in conversation that she is interested in another young man who has an expensive sports car. At that moment, the young man experiences abandonment, rejection, sadness, loss and self-doubt. It has become apparent to the young man, that he alone is not worthy of attention or affection, and that in order to receive what he desires and not risk being rebuffed in the future, he must possess an expensive sports car. His first reaction however, is the emotion of anger. He is angry at being rejected, angry at not feeling self-worth and angry at the other young man who has now been touted as being superior to him. At this point, a typical young man often takes one of two paths. In the first path, the young man becomes obsessed with obtaining a car and other material possessions, which he feels will attract the attention and admiration of young women. He becomes consumed with this obsession and once he is able to obtain and fulfill this object of his desire, he becomes filled with false pride. It is false pride because the desire was not to obtain a vehicle for love of the vehicle, but rather as a means to an end to gain power and control.

Once this is achieved, the car also becomes an attachment, because as the young man is learning through this ego trip, one must protect this attachment at all costs, as it preserves the feeling of self-worth and power and control. This in turn leads to greed, to want more and more, because the feeling of self-worth is falsely inflated and thus requires more and more acquisitions to feed the hunger within. This cycle continues, as the young man still equates feelings of acceptance and love to be based on his material possessions. Even though he may gain the admiration and companionship of the women that he originally sought, he no longer feels that he is loved for himself. He must strive daily to hold on to his possessions and maintain control, so that he can continue to have admiration and companionship. On this path, the young man is trapped in this cycle of negative reinforcement, which makes it difficult to connect with the higher self in order to explore feelings of self-love based solely on the person and the soul, rather than material possessions.

On the second path, the young man is not motivated enough to work and do what is necessary to obtain the finances needed to purchase the sports car. Faced with this decision, he instead decides to wallow in sadness and anger. He blames circumstances and others for his problems and seeks and finds people of a similar lower angry vibration, whom he finds comfort in associating himself with as companions. These like-minded people are also willing to blame the world and others for the source of their miseries, rather than accepting responsibility for their negative thoughts and poor choice of actions. This anger and detachment from other emotions and people serves to produce and further expand feelings of self-loathing. While the young man may not become attached to a material good, he becomes attached to the anger and other resulting emotions. In this scenario, anger eats away at him from the inside out and the emotions must be quieted, so the young man in many cases turns to other sources and substances to avoid the expressions and pain of these emotions.

In both cases, the ego is out of control and the person exists in a state of being dominated by the lower bodies. In a third scenario, which was taught in the mystery schools and the esoteric teachings, the young man is able to fully see this situation as it unfolds. He is able to view the experience from his higher self and understand the situation using the power of discernment. He would see the bigger picture, which reveals that he reached out originally in love to another person, in this case the young woman. The young woman herself, while appearing confident, was suffering from insecurity and did not love herself and so she believed that being with a person who had an expensive car would elevate her status and feelings of worthiness and love. The young man is able to see and connect with this situation as it is unfolding and understands that rather than taking the situation personally, that they are two people coming from two different energy fields at this moment of time on their journeys. In this scenario, the young man would simply understand the situation for what it is, and filled with self-love for himself, he would not be reactive, but rather would be able to be proactive. He would send love to this person, from a higher level unconditional love and then be free to move on to the next experience. In this mindset, the young man is able to learn from the experience and understand it further, without creating and causing a long negative chain and karmic cycle of misery and negative emotions for him and others.

In this example, we gain the knowledge that ego, while convincing us that it is protecting us, is in fact, keeping us trapped within our lower bodies. In actuality, it is blocking us from discovering our true selves. Once a Neophyte student understands this invaluable concept, it becomes easier to work through the trappings of ego and unravel them to create an ego in balance, in which the ego takes a back seat to the higher mind. When ego is in balance, discernment always comes into play first. With each experience, the person is not instantly reactive to a situation; rather they are able to process the event as it occurs around them and understand from deeper and more complex levels.

From this loving place, one is able to share their accomplishments and goals with others as forms of inspiration, rather than in a posturing or bragging state. In the balanced state, ego is used wisely to help one move forward into the creative phases of action, driving one to continue to create and explore. The major difference in this state of mind is that the focus is on the person to achieve their personal best, rather than directed as a reflection of competition tied to what others are achieving or acquiring in order to feel better.

The journey to transcend the ego, takes a dedicated amount of time and work, coupled with a willingness to truly look in the mirror and see what one has created in their lives and what walls are built around them. If this is done correctly, it is a huge undertaking and not an easy experience to face. In the mystery school teachings, it is described as a symbolic death, the death of the ego, which does indeed feel like a near death experience. Many students find that they can not move past this lesson and go no further in the teachings. They fear that if they unravel what is keeping them together, they will lose themselves and all sense of power and control over themselves and others. To do this work of transcending, most students find it helpful to have a loving teacher, who is willing to guide them through this process. It requires tremendous inner strength to take on this lesson and work through the emotions. The ego does not like to give up control and it will fight the entire way and use any means it has with the personality to maintain power and control, including convincing the student that the teacher is causing them to do something that is wrong and possibly harmful to them. This esoteric teaching has been the subject of many novels, fairy tales, parables and lessons, as it is one of the most difficult lessons for a Neophyte student to gain control over and master. It is described in its most basic stage, as taking the first leap of faith in the journey of the esoteric teachings as a Neophyte student.

Once one has gained control over their lower bodies and the ego, the higher self is able to communicate more directly with the mind, which leads to greater intuition and guidance. Note that I say greater intuition, there are some people who are able to be intuitive, accessing information from the lower planes and can access intuitive/psychic information, without having worked on the lower mind and the ego. One does not have to proceed the other in order to work, but it is found that if a person does first work on some form of either the esoteric teachings, or other spiritual teachings and on the inner self, that the psychic and intuitive abilities are able to reach into higher realms and obtain greater degrees of information for some purposes.

From the new found establishment of connection with the higher self, the ability to understand the law of attraction and how to create positive thoughts, producing positive actions returns back to you. This is one of these occasions where esoteric teachers rejoice, as they have assisted the Neophyte in "remembering one lesson which they already knew on a soul level." What is most freeing for students at this point, is the realization that if they progress beyond the controlling ego, that while they can not control every situation which occurs to them, they can control how they react to these situations, which in turn, can lead to a more satisfying, fulfilling and peaceful life. These gifts are more priceless than any material possession.

Now that a brief understanding of ego has been discussed, the knowledge of how thoughts create our reality and the control of emotions is the next most important lesson to tackle. This lesson is often misunderstood. Many students confuse the concept of control of emotions, to mean that one strives to have no emotions. This could not be further from the truth. The exact opposite is what is meant to be achieved. Energy can not be destroyed, only changed. This is a basic precept of the teachings and is understood by every esoteric student, as is the concept that you cannot not think of something while in a creative phase. If I say to you right now, "Do Not Think About A White Elephant!" What are you thinking about as you read these words?

That's right, because you can not replace thoughts in this manner. To briefly explain the lesson of the controlling of emotions, it means that one is able to fully experience each emotion with the discernment of where these emotions are coming from, why they are occurring, and what the emotions can teach the student and the other people who are affected.

One of the most dangerous ego traps for a Neophyte student is misunderstanding this lesson. Many of them pride themselves that they are not as emotional as other students and therefore this must mean that they have progressed further on the path. This is not the case, as to move from a Neophyte to an Initiate in the teachings, one must become a master of their emotions, which means not to abolish them, but rather to embrace them and allow the emotions to move through them, understanding them and other's emotions with compassion and wisdom. When one achieves full knowledge and control of the emotions, they can lead to some of the most profound experiences in life. When we are able to access the higher mind, we can use this Divine Intelligence to control our emotions by observing the experiences as they unfold around us. We allow the emotions to flow through us, without taking control over our entire being. This is a complete transformation, in comparison to how the masses of people live, which is to experience a negative event, which sets off a chemical and emotional reaction of words, thoughts, deeds and actions, which occur quickly without discerning thought. The emotional overload continues until the person is overwhelmed and exhausted by the emotions and shuts down again, before the next overwhelming experience. If this repeats often enough in a person's life, they begin to feel depleted and look for other stimulants or sources to recharge their energy, as they are unable to charge themselves through natural energy any further.

When a person grows too weary from experiencing emotions, they choose either a self defensive mechanism of blocking emotions, or they continue to drain their energy until they experience a state of depression where their emotional body has been completely exhausted. In these states, it is difficult for the body to keep up with the demands put upon it via the emotional and mental bodies. Either way is highly destructive to the person on all four bodies. If the emotions are blocked and trapped, it requires energy to keep these feelings closed, which takes away energy which would have been used for creative outlets. If the person runs through their emotions to the point of exhaustion and depression, the containment field that holds their energy fields, also known as the aura, is damaged and unable to hold in the energy as needed. At this point, the person is in effect, a leaking ship, awash in a turbulent sea of emotions.

Emotions are meant to be a powerful guide to lead each person to a deeper understanding while on the path of connecting with higher love through the heart chakra. The key is to understand that emotions are a valuable gift to us, but as with all things, we must be the wise benevolent leader who is able to compassionately control the amount of time and energy we give to them, as with all things. Emotions are energy and like all creations in existence, they communicate in one way or another. They desire to share with us what they have to teach in the form in which they are able to do this. When we can acknowledge each emotion for what it is attempting to show to us, its mission is complete. At this level of communication, emotions are able to move through us and release the energy back into the ethers. As a student understands and embraces this teaching, it is quickly seen how much less energy is expended by simply allowing the emotion to be and then pass quickly through the bodies and released, which is a much more natural way of existing.

As we become more conscious in this way, we are living in the moment, or what is called the Now. By this time, we are well on our way as a Neophyte to living life more fully, rather than being reactive and living with the fears of our past or the worries of our future.

It is important to understand that emotions are intertwined and connected with thoughts and according to what thoughts are focused on most often, the resulting emotions remain in these energy fields around each person. These emotions are gifts to us to help us understand ourselves on a deeper level, as we are in search of our true divine higher self. In this sense, as a student begins to understand that everything is energy and thusly is alive in some aspect, all things need to be fed in one form or another. While thoughts don't eat food per se, they do require energy to continue to exist. In the lower levels of our bodies, while we don't yet understand how to create these energy fields of existence, we do still subconsciously feed our thoughts with our emotions. As these thoughts grow in strength, they demand more of our attention, which demands more energy, which demands more sustenance. Are you beginning to see this unhealthy cycle of energy?

Once the thoughts have enough energy where they become a belief, they have a new level of strength and are fed daily through various thoughts and emotions being created. At this point, the person, who was first the creator of the thought, now becomes led by the thoughts which have gained enough energy from the mind to become beliefs. These beliefs then spiral into thoughts, words, deeds and actions, creating karmic effects and spiraling negative experiences. This process is so deep rooted and hidden by the ego in the subconscious that most people do not understand how they got into these situations. Even more tragic, they can not explain why they reacted a certain way about a situation at times. When pressed for an answer, they simply do not know, citing a feeling of being out of control, out of their mind for a moment and overwhelmed with emotion.

At this point, we are not creators, we are maintainers and the ego finds a comfortable spot here, spinning stories filled with delusions and preconceived ideas, dogmas and fears. If you have recognized some of these experiences within yourself, do not feel bad, for what is done can also be undone. Each person has the ability to be a creator. Once a person has realized what is happening to them, they are able to begin to remove these old patterns and beliefs and create new, positive thoughts, filled with loving emotions.

This process is not easily accomplished. It is recommended that the journey be explored with a trusted esoteric teacher or counselor to assist you with this lesson.

The path unfolds in steps including...

Stage One – A Dark and Stormy Night:

In this first stage, the student becomes aware they have a lower self and a higher self and that the circumstances in their life have led them to live most of their life with the lower self in charge. The person then begins to take a hard, deep introspective look at their life. They must see what they have created with their thoughts and emotions and make the decision to accept responsibility for their actions. They also understand the concept that they create their reality with their thoughts, words, actions and deeds and therefore can create new realities for themselves should they choose to do so. The Neophyte recognizes they have a higher consciousness/higher self and becomes aware of the purpose of ego and that they are not just the ego personality.

Stage Two – The Long Journey to Self:

The Neophyte, coming from a new connection with their higher consciousness/self understands why the ego created the patterns it did out of protection. They now understand there is a different way to approach new experiences. At this point, the student realizes that the way to reach and further activate the higher self is through self-love, compassion and discernment. Rather than beating themselves up over past choices, they see why they made these choices and why they allowed the ego and lower self to take control as a protective mechanism. They recognize they have the tools and abilities to transform their life. The urge to live a life full of experiences and growth is stronger than the urge to remain imprisoned in a wall of self-created blocks put into place by fear. The student understands that most fears are irrational and are only made stronger with the thoughts supporting and attracting this energy to them in greater waves. They understand truly through the law of attraction, that if they can change their thinking, they can change their life!

Stage Three – Embracing The Struggle and The Release:

The higher consciousness/self challenges the ego. The ego moves back into fear of loss of control and power and an ensuing struggle engages until one or the other wins. As the student begins to create change, a surprising wall of resistance appears. The ego prepares for a great battle, rising up and pulling forth every fear and control mechanism it can muster, in an attempt to scare the student into disbelieving and doubting everything they have considered up to this point. This is the breaking point for many Neophyte students, where they find that they do not feel strong enough to continue on this journey. They fear they will lose their personal power and sense of who they are, and that they will not be able to maintain or accomplish what they wish to achieve in this lifetime, without having the controlling power of the ego in charge. A part of them on some level still realizes that the ego in control does not feel peaceful, but the fear of the unknown is a greater fear for them. They find comfort in this fact and retreat. For the remaining students who push through this fear and emerge through the other side, they have just faced and won a battle that is the equivalent to winning the Spiritual Olympics. This student receives their first transformation, and a strong cord of connection is created with the higher self which stays with the person throughout their lifetime, regardless of how much further they proceed with the teachings. The accomplishment of this one lesson is a major step on the path to self-knowledge and spiritual growth and should be celebrated.

Stage Four – The Act and Art of Creating Balance:

The higher consciousness/self and creative mind is connected and becomes the leader in thoughts and emotions, which continues forward through words, thoughts, actions and deeds. The ego exists in a positive form, providing creative drive and action. The student begins to see the world through an entirely different point of view. Each person, place and experience is new again to them. Every act is inspiring, as the higher self is strongly attached to the person and able to speak more directly to the student, showing them the wonder, magic and miracles in all experiences. Each moment has a sacred energy and a sense of reverence. The student sees life again with the wonder of a child, combined with a new found wisdom and appreciation. As it is described in the bible, "Be Ye Transformed, By The Renewing of Your Mind" also expressed as, "And be not conformed to this world: but be ye transformed by the renewing of your mind, that ye may prove what is that good and acceptable, and perfect will of God." From this point of engagement, the student is able to more easily grasp the deeper peelings of the onion in the teachings and progresses further.

It is at this point, the Neophyte begins to understand a more advanced esoteric teaching which is known as a teaching within a teaching.

Known by mystery schools and alchemists, this teaching is a sacred formula:

The Power of Thought

+

The Art of Creative Visualization

=

The Universal Power of Reality

In short, the most important concept you can grasp from this lesson is that you have the power.

As Gandhi said, "Be the change you want to see in the world."

Chapter Four

Lesson Three:
We Are All One, A Sea of Energy Floating In Vibratory Fields

"Matter is Energy, Energy is Light,
We are all light beings."
-- Albert Einstein --

One of the most profound revelations a soul experiences on the Neophyte level, is when the student remembers that we are all energy beings surrounded and enveloped in various degrees of energy and motion. This coupled with the understanding that everyone is connected with the All That Is and that the All That Is, is everything, everywhere and everyone, is a mind altering experience. This is the beginning of the explanation of the deeper concepts and teachings of the body/mind/spirit connection.

An entire book can be dedicated to the further explanation of any of these lessons, as the depth and breadth of each subject is most extensive. The best we can accomplish in this book is to give the interested student a brief overview of these Neophyte teachings in order to stimulate the mind and stir the soul into reaching for more information.

In the teachings of universal energy, the scientific world of physics is beginning to explain energy and matter and further expound on the ancient teachings of many cultures and mystics who have explained that we are all stardust and that our bodies are comprised from the materials of the universe. We will focus here on how this particular teaching, affects you in your body, as it is best to be introduced first to the concepts and learn to master them within oneself first, before moving outward again.

One of the most important lessons regarding our bodies of energy is the understanding that there is an energy field which surrounds our body. This is known as the aura. All living things have auras, including plants, animals and humans. The aura can be seen by humans and with practice I have found that all of my students have been able to see an aura around a person to some degree.

Some students are resistant at first about the concept and importance of the aura, and so I teach about the aura with this lesson. There is a universal force described in the eastern teachings as chi and in the western teachings as universal energy. This chi/energy spirals, some compare it to a DNA molecule. The energy travels downward from the sun, moon, planets, and stars and upwards from the earth, ocean, plants and trees. We are all born with our own personal chi, which begins when we take our first breath at birth. The most profound statement that I could ever teach anyone, and I could spend decades teaching this one statement in greater detail is:

The Breath is The Life.

We will discuss this further in a later chapter.

Our chi is unique and emanates within and throughout us as energy. With each breath we draw inward, we bring in the existing chi around us. With each exhale, we release this chi back to the universe. Let's think about this for a moment.

The chi which we breathe in, is taken from the air closest around us.

When the Neophyte student truly understands that chi is pure energy charged with the positive or negative sources we create around us, the awareness of how important one's thoughts and emotions are become overwhelmingly important. The student sees they are breathing back in the energy they are creating!

This energy is being circulated around the person and is the energy field which is emanating from them. This is an important lesson, as it also further explains the law of attraction and how the energy you have created in your auric field is the first thing which is felt by other people, even when you walk into a room.

As an example, have you ever met someone for the first time and felt that this person was unhappy, spiteful, or angry before you even said a word to them? This is because their emotions are spilling forth from inside them and swirling outward around them. In this state, as they are releasing or fuming with anger, they are breathing in the negatively charged air they are creating which serves to add fuel to the fire. It is easy to understand then how one can create and then be trapped in a repetitive cycle of thinking and then feel unable to snap out of that feeling.

Take depression for example. The person becomes depressed over a period of time. As they become depressed, their thoughts are attracted to this mood, and their energy is low. They feel fatigued, lethargic and tend to breathe very shallow. As their depressed thoughts extend outward from them, they continue to breathe in the same negatively charged chi. The cycle continues until something is altered to charge the air differently. The severity of the depression defines how easily or difficultly the air and mood is lifted. A person, who is feeling down because of the loss of a job or a love interest, may snap out of their feelings after a few weeks because of an incredible job offer they receive or meeting a new person. A person with deeper depression may require help from other sources such as a therapist to help them review and alter their thoughts and emotions. In some cases, medication is used to alter the chemical balance which has been created within the body due to the long term downward spiral of thoughts. The prescription in this case, can create a barrier between the physical and emotional fields, which serves to disconnect the energy temporarily from the emotional body where the energy was being created which led to the depression. In these cases, medication should be combined with additional therapeutic assistance to help the person search within themselves and renew their awareness of hope and purpose. This in turn, gives them the strength to move forward with revitalized positive thoughts and emotions which subconsciously renews chi and recharges their energy.

If you think about these examples for a moment, you will recall old sayings still in use today. After a fight, someone might say, we need to clear the air or someone who has been working too hard might say, I need a breath of fresh air, a vacation away. Or when something just doesn't feel right, but you can't place your finger on what it is, you might say, there's something in the air.

Our chi emanates outside of our body in the auric force field which encompasses our body. Learning about the aura of one's own body, as well as others can be very helpful in many ways. The aura can indicate the health of the body as well as the condition of the mind and soul.

As the Neophyte student begins to learn about their aura, they are taught a series of lessons including how to determine if their aura is healthy and vibrant, or whether it is has become frail. They learn to determine whether or not their aura is leaking energy or has a spongy texture to it which must be repaired. The student is taught how to build up the energy of their aura and how to form an impenetrable white light shield around their body as needed in certain situations.

I describe auras to my students as "emotions in motion." When you see a person's aura, and its many colors, you are seeing their current thoughts and vibrations. The fields of the aura can grow and expand. For some people, this is a temporary expansion, which occurs when they are highly excited, or experiencing energetic emotions of anger and fear or love and joy. Students who work with the various fields of their bodies, can sense when their aura expands and becomes healthier. In addition, they can feel the influence and energy of a person through their aura.

For example, do you know a person who is warm, dynamic and attracts attention wherever they go? A person whom complete strangers open up to, feeling relaxed and desiring to be in this person's company? If yes, then you have found a person with a strong, healthy aura.

As Neophyte students begin to work on their aura, there are areas which need to be restored. Because the aura is affected by our thoughts, emotions and energy, it has been bombarded with our constant influx of fears, anxiety and emotional outbursts. This brings us back to the understanding of the lower self and living in a state of fear. Remember how when people live in a state of fear, in one reflection or another, they choose to build up walls or live in anger? Well, these creations also exist in the aura as well. Many students will disagree at first, stating they do not have walls and they are not angry. However, as they progress through the teachings, it is revealed that anger comes in many forms, including passive outlets which are not as easily recognized including depression, delusion and detachment. These examples along with many other walls are built daily through the thoughts and emotions.

The healthy state of an auric field should surround the body with some elasticity. We can compare this in a sense, to a filter. When a filter is clean, it maintains a natural flow and is porous, allowing air or water to move freely in and out from it as it functions and does its job. When too much debris becomes attached to the filter, it clogs up and water or air is not able to pass through as easily.

When we produce a high level of negative energy for an extended period of time, either of our making through our thoughts and emotions, or by experiences we are living through, our auric field clogs with this energy. This eventually hardens into clumps around our body. These blockages make it difficult for energy to pass in and out from the body.

This achieves the goal for the person who wanted a wall around them, as the more they strengthen these thoughts, the stronger the wall and the less that reaches them on their mental and emotional bodies. This sounds great at first, until one realizes that this also means that good energy is also not able to come through to the body. The auric field relies on nourishment, and the wall blocks the nourishment from coming inside to help the soul. Thus the energy is not able to easily recycle and flow back outward to release through the aura. Like a clogged filter, the problem continues to grow. The person is unable to receive the energy they need to pull in restorative positive light or release the negative energy.

As the aura becomes more and more clogged over time, it is unable to function as it should. The self-imposed walls continue to form and harden. The end result is that the person feels more and more disconnected from the world and other people. This in turn, affects the soul and higher self tremendously, as it is pushed farther away from what it came back to the earth plane to do. The outside of the aura continues to receive energy from the universe, but because it can not penetrate through the field into the body it surrounds, it dries up and coagulates around the auric shell. Cracks are created in this shell, forming around the weak parts of the aura. The remaining energy leaks through these cracks, removing further energy from the person. This creates a negative cycle of energy loss and decreased ability to fully replenish the body.

Hardened auras are caused by living in fear. When people seek to control other people or situations, from either an active-aggressive stance or a passive-aggressive place, the outcome is still the same. The only difference is the way a person chooses to express this energy via extroverted (attacking people directly with energy), or introverted (manipulating other's energy in a variety of ways). When there is a focus on getting even, making someone feel bad (revenge) or when we become obsessed with others actions, a hardened aura will result. An important lesson that many students must face, is that if you have the thought, it is as damaging as the action. Many students first come into the classes, believing they are superior, because they judge people with their thoughts, but do not vocalize these thoughts outwardly. They believe they are better than the students who express their thoughts verbally. This is not the case, both are equally damaging to the individual and others. Almost anyone can testify to the fact that a disapproving look by a person can hurt as much as someone who speaks the thought out loud. In fact, many people express in their relationships that they would prefer to argue and have some form of communication with a partner, rather than to suffer icy stares and the silent treatment. No one likes to be ignored and made to feel that they are not worth speaking to and being heard.

We also turn this energy on ourselves and self-destruct in fear as well. Examples of this include: when we expend precious vital energy second guessing outcomes, or planning to the minutest details, or worrying about what may happen in the future and living in regret of the past. These hardened auras are created when we live in anger, worry, doubt, control, jealousy and greed. Each time these thoughts are activated, the aura struggles further to maintain its field and it can not handle the resulting emotional and mental stress. It is being pushed to the point of an eruption, so the aura cracks further under the pressure, creating a negative spiraling cycle of further damage. If left in this condition for too long, the person becomes "hardened" as does their auric body.

In cases of depression, a person does not build up a wall to block out their feelings. However, because they are overwhelmed by their emotions, they lose their will, and this can create what is best described as a spongy aura. This aura feels a bit like quicksand, it is very porous and when viewed, resembles a squishy sea sponge or Swiss cheese. Intuitive's, who are sensitive to these energy fields, describe it as a sensation of being sucked into this person's aura. Others who are not aware of the energy fields, still experience the drain of energy. They come away from spending time with this person feeling physically drained and exhausted. When this type of auric condition continues to expand and is not corrected, the person subconsciously becomes what is known as an energy vampire. Most times they are not aware of their condition. They are struggling with their sadness and literally drowning in a sea of emotion in which they feel out of control. Their aura is in pain, and is reaching out like a person who is drowning as it tries to regain enough energy to heal itself. As it works to connect with another's energy, it begins to absorb their energy and does not know when to stop, which causes the sucking effect that one feels.

In no case is it a good idea to allow a person with a spongy aura to suck from your aura, there are much better ways to assist them.

One of the most difficult challenges an esoteric student faces, is the understanding that in most cases, people have to heal themselves from the inside out. That is why in some cases, no matter how much time, energy or care one person gives to another, it is never enough for some people. This is due to the fact that without self-love, it is difficult for a person to believe the positive thoughts and energy directed toward them. The most healing act one can ever do for another person is to send them love. The most healing act one can do to heal oneself, is to love oneself. Love in the highest levels, comes in many forms, including compassion, patience, empathy, and kindness. All of these should come from the higher self, tempered with discernment and wisdom. When love is sent from the higher self, it can stimulate the energy field around the person, giving them additional strength to break down the walls around their auric field. Love can also assist with repairing a spongy aura, encouraging the person to gain control over their emotions.

Love is the greatest power that exists, period

Neophyte students are taught how to gain control over their emotions. The lessons explain how each person creates and chooses to feel the emotions presented to them each day. They begin to realize that when they live life as an over-emotional person, they are not just the person drowning, but also the stormy sea.

Energy Cords

Once the Neophyte student has a firm grasp on understanding the auric field, they are then taught about cords which can attach from one person to another energetically. In the teachings, this is taught so that Initiate students can communicate with each other telepathically.

One of the examples that I like to share with my students was taught to me while I was in the beautiful state of Hawaii. While there, I was able to spend some time with an amazing teacher who shared some of the Huna teachings. The teachers of Huna, known as Kahuna's, teach the sacred esoteric teachings to their students orally. These teachings have advanced level esoteric knowledge which is kept secret until the student has done the work and has proven that they would only use this information for the purest of intentions. As with all esoteric teachings, those advanced teachings must be passed on directly from teacher to student in the oral fashion, as it is a complex system of energy and connecting on multiple levels which require a direct link and experience.

The lesson that I would like to speak of here though, is one that is taught on the basic level and is shared with Neophytes at most mystery schools. This is the lesson of the etheric threads and cords. Each person has a series of cords which extend from their body. Western esoteric students are familiar with some of these cords as they are referred to in the teachings with their various purposes, including the silver cord.

The threads extend from each of us like network cables which communicate and provide a variety of functions, including delivering vital energies to the body and as conduits bringing thoughts to the body. Some threads are used more often than others and the more attention which is brought to a thread and the more often it is used, the thread grows thicker and stronger until it has the strength of a cord.

The Huna teaching which I mentioned earlier describes this in such beautiful teachings. One of my favorite is that of a handshake. The teaching is as follows: When physical contact (a handshake, hug or more intimate contact) is made between two people, an etheric thread is attached between them, which remains connected to the two people throughout their lifetime. The strength of this thread is heightened or lessened depending upon how much thought, energy or interaction you spend with the person. Remember when business deals were made on the strength of a handshake? This was strengthened as both partners looked each other in the eye and gave their word, which was sealed with a handshake. This was considered as strong as any written contract. This was powerful, as these agreements were made between two people with strong auric fields who understood what they were agreeing to and what it meant. This is why in so many native and indigenous cultures, written contracts were completely unnecessary, words mean so little in comparison to a connection on this level. The individuals were fully aware of what this meant and the karmic repercussions of going back on their word.

Going back to this connection, as you engage your energy with another person through a handshake, embrace or other means of physical contact, your energy and thoughts are shared more with them through each contact, as are your emotions. The other person in return, shares their energy with you. The more attention focused on this person, the stronger the threads become until it grows into a strong cord. Is there no wonder that the strong bond between families is referred to as family ties? Perhaps there is also more to the example that nature teaches us, when a child is born and has received its nourishment for nine months through the umbilical cord and years later when the child leaves home as an adult, people remind the parents that the time had come to cut the cord.

As this energy develops, most of humanity recognizes this connection in one form or another. Parents will describe their willingness to do anything for their children, spouses after spending years together are told that they have begun to look similar to each other and finish each others sentences. With esoteric students, they are taught how to use these cords further, to establish telepathic communication with others whom they wish to be strongly connected. Many women develop this naturally in its beginning stages as they sense what is called women's intuition, and can feel how their children are doing, even when they are far away. Another example is the awareness a woman feels when a spouse is pulling away from them energetically.

There are hundreds of lessons which are taught to esoteric students on auric fields and how they can be of great use to the student and to others. The study of auras and what they mean is a long term lesson for the Neophyte student and continues into the other esoteric levels. One fascinating example is the story related by Edgar Cayce, who was in a high rise office building waiting for an elevator to return him to the first floor. When the elevator opened in front of him, he was astonished as he could not see the aura of any person on the elevator. This surprised him, as he was used to seeing the auric field around people wherever he went. In his puzzlement, he did not enter into the elevator. The elevator closed and the cable of the elevator snapped, plummeting all of the people on the elevator to their death. As the body prepares for the death process, the auric field prepares the way for the body to move from one plane of existence into the next, pulling inward, rather than outward, which is what he viewed that day.

Neophyte students learn many lessons on the death process, including what occurs during the death process and how certain cords are released from the body in stages.

The aura is described to students as we have iterated as emotions in motion and as such, is a constantly changing field. Some colors and energy remain in the aura for longer periods of time and this is due to the thoughts and energy which are consistently being fed to the aura. Good psychics understand this energy and this is some of what they are picking up when they are reading a person. Remember, each person is a creator and their thoughts create their reality. For most people, their thoughts remain fairly consistent, which then creates this energy in their fields, bringing this reality to them. Psychics are able to access and read these fields, which shows them the potential outcome of what is to come in your future. This is why psychics will explain that this reading is based only on what they see at this moment. Due to the concept of free will, a person has the ability to change their thoughts at any time, which would then alter the outcome of their future.

Many esoteric students were unaware of how this level of psychic ability works until they studied the lessons of the auric bodies and how thoughts are formed and created.

Restoration of the Auric Field

The easiest way to begin to restore your aura is to have a deep and restful sleep. This restores what is described as the pranic energy. As students develop, their aura becomes healthy and strong. A good night's sleep will refresh their energy and they are ready to go again the next day. However, for most people, they have been wrestling with their thoughts and emotions for years and their aura has been depleted in some fashion. In addition, if they have been under a long period of stress or worry or illness, it will take much longer to restore the auric field as the body has to repair itself on many levels. This concept was understood in the past, much more than it is understood today. It was not so long ago when doctors offered prescriptions to their patients with the advice: retire to the country or the seaside for a period of three months, to restore vitality to the body. Many patients found that fresh air and removal from the stressful energy of the city did wonders to restore their health and their mood. This period of rest and relaxation also gave the auric field time to repair and restore as well.

This advice is still as valuable today as it always has been, however, it is more difficult today to convince people of the necessity of caring for and recharging their energetic fields. In the race to have and acquire more possessions, a huge disconnect is created, pushing the higher self further away from being able to connect with and guide the lower self. Perhaps this has something to do with the overwhelming number of people suffering from neurological disorders, anxiety attacks, insomnia and depression. Life is meant to be lived in balance and the Neophyte student soon understands that health, happiness and quality of life depends upon the balance and harmony of all of these bodies.

Besides a good night's sleep, another powerful way of restoring energy to the auric fields is by the active prayer of bringing white light around the energy fields. This focuses energy and draws it into the body and each of the energetic fields at the same time. The process of this prayer raises the vibrations within the person and activates vital energy. This stimulation excites the higher self and calls it forth to send greater energy to all parts of the body.

To bring forth the White Light Energy, follow these instructions:

1. Cleanse and prepare your body, by first taking a shower. While in the shower, visualize the water cleansing your body as well as the auric field surrounding your body. If you are experiencing any negative thoughts or emotions, release them while in the shower, allowing them to dissipate and dissolve in the water.

2. Dry your body and remain naked if possible. If this is not possible, wear loose clothing made of natural fibers, (no man made materials). Find a quiet and private area of your home and sit comfortably in a position where your arms and legs are unencumbered and your posture is such that you can breathe deeply and easily without obstruction.

3. Close your eyes and begin by taking a deep breath inward to the count of three. Hold the breath for the count of three and then release the breath to the count of three. After this first inhale and exhale, take the next breath, following the same count, except during this inhale, visualize beautiful clear air coming into you. Hold the breath for the count of three. Visualize this breath gathering up any negative energy inside of you. When you exhale this time, exhale fully from the mouth, blowing out the negative energy. Repeat this process one more time.

4. Now you are ready to draw in the white light. Some people like to light a white candle to assist them in this process. Close your eyes and visualize the pure white light of the universal energy. See this white light drawing closer to you. Once you can effectively visualize the white light around you, it is time to take a deep breath again to the count of three. On this deep inward breath, draw in the white light through your nostrils bringing it deep inside of you. While holding the breath to the count of three, feel the light circulating and spiraling throughout your body. This time when you exhale, release the white light through the top of your head (crown chakra) while exhaling through the mouth. Repeat this breath exercise three times.

5. At the end of each of these breath cycles of inhale, hold and exhale, then say aloud:

    The White Light of Universal Love Surrounds Me,
    The White Light of Universal Love Surrounds Me,
    The White Light of Universal Love Surrounds Me.

    And only that which is for my Highest and Best
    Is Made Manifest Through to Me.

    I ask for Divine Order, Divine Wisdom, and Divine Guidance.

    I Give Thanks, I Give Thanks, I Give Thanks!

6. Neophyte students are taught to raise their arms in the air (forming the shape of a large V) while performing these breathing exercises and prayers. The arms remain extended in the air during the entire exercise. When the exercise is complete, the student crosses their arms across their chest, as is seen in the burial rituals of ancient Egypt. This act locks the energy into the body and seals the aura.

7. The prayer given above is the generic form of the prayer. Depending upon a student's religious preferences it can be substituted to say I am sur-rounded by the Pure White Light of the Christ or Angels etc. The energy lies not as much in the words stated, as it is the energy which is felt, expressed and drawn in during this prayer ritual.

When done as a regular practice, (Neophytes are asked to complete this ritual at the beginning and end of their day), students quickly discover that the energy fields of their body begin to hum with renewed vigor and vitality. Almost every student will report a difference in their lives as they begin to work with this prayer, including feelings of increased energy, more positive thoughts, and less emotional reactions. They also notice that people around them begin to comment on how they feel and appear different to them.

If this prayer is done consistently, combined with the work of daily house-keeping to clear the mind of negative thoughts and emotions, the Neophyte quickly accelerates on their journey. These two processes work best hand in hand, as it is difficult and time wasting, to draw in powerful light energy if it is only going to be quickly dissipated by negative thoughts and emotions and released back quickly into a cracked or spongy aura.

Chapter Five

Lesson Four:
We Are A Reflection, A Microcosm of the Macrocosm

"A sense of humor, my dear Pilgrim is a precious gift indeed,
for it is synonymous with a tuned-in intellect, and a highly evolved mind
as well as with spiritual profundity. Know that there can be no wisdom
where there is no humor and while all those with humor do not contain wisdom,
they possess the initial sparks, conversely all those with wisdom do possess humor.
For there can be no wisdom where there is no humor and no healing laughter.
A sense of the ridiculous is a necessity for enlightenment which is why Buddha
chuckles. It would behoove you to always keep in mind to beware of a man or a
woman who is unable to laugh at himself, or at herself or at the entire Universal
pattern of existence. For humor you see, has as its foundation,
a true and deep perception of both the human and the galactic condition
revealing the person who possesses it to also possess infinite compassion
and above all, a sense of perfect balance."
-- Linda Goodman, astrologer --

Dear student, as you have progressed this far, it is no surprise to you when we state that we are part of the whole and the whole is part of us! This is an ancient esoteric teaching which is known as: As Above, So Below.

In the grand scale conceptual teachings, the axiom, As Above, So Below explains the existence of the duality of the seen and unseen worlds as they exist in a mirrored reflection of each other. What happens in one world has a similar reaction in the other world. What is Above, the Universe, is reflected Below, on the Earth. The Divine Spirit Above, is reflected Below in Hu-man.

To gain understanding of this concept, we begin with the "below", which is our body on the earth plane. We have already learned that we create in our bodies, with our thoughts, words, actions and deeds which affect us and the world around us through the law of attraction. Now we expand upon this lesson, with the understanding that these same thoughts, words, actions and deeds also affect the spiritual planes above us.

To begin this lesson, the Neophyte student is taught to focus on the four bodies closest to their physical body, which are the etheric body, astral/emotional body, mental body and the intuitional/spiritual body. These bodies are the ones in which they are most affected by on a regular basis. It is not possible to explain in the confines of this book how each of these bodies work. We will attempt here though to introduce examples of how they affect one at the Neophyte level.

For example, each thought we have in our mind, is then reflected throughout these bodies and released upward into the higher planes. The job of these planes is to take action on each thought and create the energy to accomplish this thought. These planes receive the energy without judgment or discernment.

They simply are responsive to the energy and act upon the intent of the energy.

These bodies can only help deliver the messages they receive from your thoughts and emotions. The Neophyte student understands that if they think about something hard enough and long enough, they will attract it to themselves. Many people, who are not esoteric students, have also been taught this concept at some level. However, in the esoteric teachings, this is considered to be teaching only part one of the lesson.

The most important part of the lesson which should be taught in the beginning is:

Be careful what you wish for, as you just might receive it!

When an esoteric student engages in these lessons, they are taught the value of discernment and connection with the higher self. When a student can speak through their higher self, they can ask for Divine Order and for their Highest and Best, rather than just what they wish to receive in the moment. This leads to an entirely different type of experience, as it connects the higher self fully into this action, rather than just sheer force of will, using thought to bring forth the law of attraction. Can you see the difference and how the outcomes might be very different in this case?

Before deciding that you will use the power of will and the law of attraction to bring something to you, ponder this first: Try to make sense of why you have chosen to live this life the way you have, and where you are now.

Then, ask yourself the most important question that an esoteric student can answer:

Who Are You?

If you find you can not answer this question at this time, begin by asking yourself the questions presented here in this lesson. In order to help you further understand and unravel who you are at the core of your being, take your time and carefully consider each and every question.

Are you living for yourself or to please others?
Do you know there's more to life, but not sure how to find it?
When was the last time you asked yourself these questions?
What was your answer?
Was it your answer or did another person provide you with the answers?
Did the answers come from deep inside of you?
What part of you is answering?
Do the answers change and fluctuate depending upon the mood you are in?
What do you want most out of life and why?
Do you like the person you see in the mirror today?
Why are you here?

The answer to these questions can not be explained or answered in one or two lessons. The fact is, these lessons can only give you a hint as to why each of us are here.

At this stage of study, the Neophyte student becomes acutely aware of why the esoteric teachings have traditionally always been for the few. It is not because as some may think, that there is a desire to keep it away from the masses. Rather, it is that it takes a precious amount of vital energy to truly teach and to study these lessons. At any given time, there are typically only a few people who are willing to do the introspection necessary to know and understand who they are on every level of their being.

Let's return to the discussion of As Above, So Below. Our body is a delicate and complex chemical concoction of solid matter including bones, muscles, organs and tissue, working in tandem with various liquids including blood, water, acids, bile and other products and gases created through various functions. These chemical reactions create matter not only in the dense physical body, but in the fields outside of the body. In these fields, we have electric energy carrying currents which have stored the energy of our thoughts, along with transmitters which release and receive light. We also have storage packs which have the ability to hold longer lasting energy (prana) which is connected to our breath. Initiates study these lessons in depth, comparing this knowledge of as within, so without. As our organs, glands and electrical systems function within the body, there are similar functions in the other bodies and fields.

Prana is also a creation of vital energy and an entire book could be dedicated to what prana is and how it can create miraculous effects for the body mind and spirit on all of the planes. At the Neophyte level however, we focus on introductory teachings here, thus we will speak of a basic form of prana, which is stimulated through the breath.

In our physical body, the heart is the leader in charge of your body. The heart is the pumping station, and it moves the energy in the form of the blood throughout the body in the lower physical sense. In the higher esoteric understanding, the blood carries bits of information inside of it which are received from the other bodies. This message is delivered throughout the body, instructing it from a higher level of what the person has asked for via their thoughts and emotions.

Wow! Think about this for a moment.

Every thought and emotion you have,
is recorded in the various bodies.
An imprint of that recording is in your blood,
which pumps through every organ and artery in your body.

Take a moment here and ask yourself,

What messages have you been sending to your heart?
What energy does your heart receive from you?

We all understand that if the heart decides to stop working, nothing else matters in the physical body at that point. One day people will understand how important it is that we pay attention to the stress levels we are under and the life we are choosing to live. In time, people will understand why it is so important for each person to answer the question, Who Am I?

When a person lives in conflict with their lower and higher selves, (working in a career where they are unhappy or living a life in which they are not vibrating at the right frequency for who they are meant to be), conflict is the result in all of the bodies including the physical body. The result is reflected as dis-ease.

I hope you are beginning to understand dear student that even what we are explaining to you here on this one level, is but a tiny microcosm of the macrocosm of the esoteric teachings and these levels of existence. We can but discuss only a small amount of these teachings in one book, yet if you take the time to re-read these teachings again and meditate upon them, more will be revealed to you as you reflect on these words, as you peel back this layer of the onion.

As Edgar Cayce explained, "Electricity or vibration is that same energy, same power, ye call God. Not that God is an electric light or an electric machine, but a vibration, that is creative; that is of the same energy as life itself."

Returning back to this study of the physical body, it is hard at work, creating energy, gathering energy, releasing energy and attracting energy to it as well. Various parts of the body have stronger connections to the higher planes, the heart of course having the strongest connection, followed by the brain and the vital organs. The energy field surrounding the physical body, works to protect the body from energy which could come as too much of a jolt to the body. The physical body works hand in hand with the other bodies, in almost every function.

An example of this is when the body is in what is described as a state of shock. In this state, the protective field around the body, (the etheric body) attempts to absorb the impact of this energy as much as it can, to protect the heart and organs from directly receiving the jarring impact of this information. Of course, if we have put our body and the surrounding fields under too much stress and bombarded them over time with too many negative thoughts or emotions, these fields are weakened and can not absorb the energy for very long. In these cases, the energy slips through at rapid speed, attacking the organs with great velocity. Any organ which is already weakened, through genetics or other means, is less able to withstand the blow and can be affected. We hear stories such as: the news came as a blow to them; or they could not take the news, and suffered a stroke or heart attack.

Other people experience this stress by being affected in their nervous systems. This is displayed in the physical body with the symptoms of digestive disorders, anxiety, nervous breakdowns and depression. As the student learns how each field is intertwined and connected, they understand that their thoughts truly are not secret. Their thoughts and emotions have a direct effect on all parts of them, from the inside and out and there is no hiding these thoughts. Whether you decide to consciously create or not, the thoughts will continue and they will work to build strong or weak systems around you each day. The good news is that the thoughts you give the most energy to, are the thoughts which grow the strongest. Once the student is aware of this valuable knowledge, they can begin to change their life in any direction that they would like to go by changing their thoughts.

In the esoteric teachings, Neophyte students are given comprehensive knowledge and understanding of the astral/emotional body and the mental body. These teachings are of great importance, because until the Neophyte can gain control of their thoughts and emotions, they can not alter this body.

It is also worth noting at this point, that whenever we discuss the bodies, planes and energy fields, including the auric field, that further esoteric study should be included at the same time of all of the chakras. Chakras are twirling vortex's of energy which gather energy at the appropriate levels and if in balance, serve to assist all of the bodies in creating positive energy at all of these levels. If the bodies or fields are overwhelmed or out of balance, the chakras are affected as well and are unable to spin as they should to be of use in their highest functions.

In the workshops I teach, I often have people come up to me who wish for me to help them to balance their chakras and cleanse their auras. I explain to them that while I can assist them on that day to do both, that it would be an extremely temporary repair.

This is because until the person works to clear their thoughts and emotions on a more permanent level, they will quickly pollute the auric field and the chakras within a few minutes of leaving a session with me. It does little good to cleanse the vessel that holds the energy if the person will leave the temple and take the vessel back outside only to fill it with mud and debris once again.

This is why so many treatments of the new age variety prove to be ineffective for people. Until it is explained to the person, that they must heal from the inside out in order for any treatment to be effective, the results will be short acting. Many healers and teachers do try to explain this at some level to the people they work with, but most do not fully comprehend the meaning when it is explained to them.

Years ago, I worked as a psychic. Before I began a reading, I would explain to the person that what I would be seeing was a path that the person was currently heading towards, due to their thoughts and actions. I explained that while I would discuss this path with them, they also had the option to change this direction at any moment. I wanted to help them to understand that they had been given one of the rarest gifts in this world, which is the gift of free will. Free will gives one the ability to alter or change an outcome. I explained to clients that they had the choice to make this change at any time, if they did not like where their future was taking them.

The majority of people I read for, always tried to rush me through this part, saying "Yes, I understand," without really understanding. They wanted to have no part in being responsible for their actions and future. They simply wanted me to tell them what was going to happen and they hoped it would be good. It is for this reason that I stopped doing psychic readings. The actions of the people reaffirmed to me, that I while I had this ability (which can be helpful), I was first and foremost a teacher. I would rather practice the old parable, "Give a man a fish and he eats for a day, teach a man to fish and he eats for a lifetime." It was during this time I realized I would teach esoteric teachings to those who were ready and had the eyes in which to see and the ears in which to hear.

In the deeper teachings, the student is taught about the astral body and how it can be strengthened through the activation of the conscious mind. At this level, the astral body is created stronger through the control of the emotions. As this body develops, esoteric students who progress to the Initiate and Adept levels begin to learn how to astral project these bodies and travel to other places. As the student develops this control, it is first seen in the dream state, where they begin to be aware, awake in a sense in their dreams, and can practice altering their dreams as they are occurring. The next stage is beginning to astral travel and future progressions lead to what I describe to my students as going to night school. This is where the astral form travels to the higher planes while the body sleeps. The student engages with other spiritual beings to learn and develop their higher self and soul further. Many schools view the astral body as a diamond in the rough for humanity, that it is in the process of transcending and evolving to take an even larger role for each person to help them in this age of evolvement for all of humanity.

The next plane around the body is the mental plane. As esoteric students soon discover, there is not just one level to any of the teachings. In addition, there is not just one level for each of these planes of existence. For the sake of these Neophyte teachings, we are only describing each of these planes here due to their complexity. It would be difficult at best to explain these teachings in their full expression and entirety in this chapter.

In the teaching of the mental plane, we share that the mind has many functions. Two of the most important functions include: the logical thought process (detail oriented) which organizes the thoughts and ideas in order so that we can replicate these concepts in the physical world, and the creative thought process, (big picture oriented) which is where ideas and inspirations are first formed, created and expressed.

When a student begins to create from their conscious mind, they understand how to use both parts of the mind to first create and image the ideas that they wish to see and then how to organize and build these ideas into a physical reality. To effectively accomplish this, the Neophyte student must learn how to clear the mental plane, so that it has the best opportunity to reach the most inspired thoughts, which is the most important part of the creative process.

Once the student has been divinely inspired, it becomes easier for the lower mind to create the logical steps to accomplish this visionary goal. Clearing the path of the mental plane is created by all of the steps we have discussed thus far in this book including building and strengthening this plane with positive energy, thoughts and emotions.

Imagine the possibilities, now that one is aware of how important thoughts and emotions are and what effects they have on every facet of life. How valuable is this information and how far reaching are the possibilities that can be brought forth.

It is at this point, that the Neophyte student begins to understand the teaching,

"Know Ye Not, That Ye Are Creators?"

The fourth plane is the intuitional plane. This is the plane where the Muses are rumored to reside. When people access this plane they receive enlightened information from the higher realms. This is the plane in which we will actually speak the least about in this introductory book. To spend time in the intuitional plane and even in the mental plane is best done in study first with a teacher. The potential exists to become wrapped up in reaching these planes without first having achieved the steps necessary to have the best energy and discernment when accessing these planes. Many students forget that the question is not always "Can I do this?", but rather, "Am I prepared to do this?"

A good esoteric teacher will spend a great amount of time working with and preparing their student before they teach them how to access these planes. They will also agree to accompany the student on their journey when possible. If any part of the ego of the student is still in control, rather than submissive while attempting this journey, the results can be disastrous and great twisting and manipulation can occur. The journey, while experienced on some level will not have the desired experience or outcome. All wisdom teachings of this nature can not be rushed; there are no shortcuts which provide the deeply desired outcome. Some students will attempt to access these planes from other directions in their desire to know, but the effects are short lived and take their toll on the person as well.

However, when the student is fully prepared and ready, connecting with the intuitional plane is an amazing experience. When the Initiate experiences this moment, it is almost indescribable, words simply won't do it justice. I refer to this as an experience teaching, which must be shared between the teacher and student who has journeyed through this level and received great insights to share in the moment.

This book is meant to serve as a guide and introduction to some of the basic concepts of the teachings with the intent to educate and inform. If at this stage of the book, you are beginning to feel overwhelmed with this information, know that you can proceed at a time that is right for you. You will know if and when this path is the right journey for you.

Remember, there are simple acts you can do each day, which greatly enhance all of your bodies and fields, directly affecting them all. One of the most effective and healing acts is to Laugh! In all seriousness, laughter is as they say the best medicine. Laugh daily; don't take yourself or the world too seriously. Laugh with abandon and joy; delight in the simple things in life, Laugh!

Should you find yourself getting caught up in the struggles of life and wondering what others are thinking, doing and saying, remind yourself that these things truly are not important and at best are distractions along the way.

As Carl Sagan has said, "The world is so exquisite, with so much love and moral depth, that there is no reason to deceive ourselves with pretty stories for which there's little good evidence. Far better, it seems to me, in our vulnerability, is to look Death in the eye and to be grateful every day for the brief but magnificent opportunity that life provides."

In addition, think positive thoughts, be happy, watch light-hearted shows, read uplifting books, don't focus on self. Give to others with joy and without thought of reciprocation, whether it be love, time or positive energy. Don't wallow in your "stuff," get up and do something, anything else. Don't allow worry and fear to creep in, banish them as soon as you notice they are trying to set up house. Face things head on and deal with them, say the White Light prayer, and think of things to be grateful for everyday. Don't hold grudges, rewrite your thoughts and let go of your past, it's over. In short, as the song says, "Don't Worry, Be Happy." If you do nothing else but change your life with these steps, your life will be altered in a dramatic fashion for the good!

Chapter Six

Lesson Five:
We Are Greater Than We Remember Ourselves To Be

"Far better it is to dare mighty things,
to win glorious triumphs even though checkered by failure,
than to rank with those poor spirits who neither enjoy nor suffer much
because they live in the gray twilight that knows neither victory nor defeat."
-- Theodore Roosevelt --

"Man Know Thyself." This axiom was taught in the ancient mystery temples of Greece. In essence, what this means is that to know oneself, is to understand the true nature of one's lower and higher self. We have also referred to this understanding with the concept of "As Above, So Below." We are the creator of our thoughts, which in turn, create our world. Man, Know Thyself is another way of stating the question we continue to discuss on a deeper level in each chapter, which is, Who Am I?

To know oneself, the Neophyte student begins by working on the lessons shared thus far in this book. It would be difficult to have worked on all of these lessons and not experienced at least some form of self-enlightenment. At the very least, one has the awareness of the higher self and soul. This begins with the esoteric understanding of not just the physical body and mind and how they work, but also the thoughts and emotions. It continues with the energy fields, bodies and planes which surround the body, reflecting and charging this energy. By now, the student begins to marvel at how much they didn't know. The concept that they've only just begun to unravel the mysteries and peel back a layer or two of onion, further excites them as they have an inkling of what the universe has to offer and share with them.

There are many parables and stories which do their best to teach about the creation of hu-man and how it all began on Earth. The most interesting part in all of these stories is usually what is described as some sort of fall. In the beginning, it is said that man was not separate in the way that humans feel separated from the source at this juncture. This sounds tragic, like something terrible occurred. What if I were to share with you instead, that it was the beginning of the most wonderful birth the universe has ever seen!

The concept begins with the knowledge that we are part of the All-mighty Universe and were created in this image and reflection. Many glorious things have been created by the Almighty Universe, the All That Is, the Universal Mind, but can you name one other creation which was given the power of free will?

Animals have thoughts and emotions, but they fall under what is known as a group soul category. In this group soul, they operate in an instinctive pattern which guides them as to what they should do in various situations. In the same respect, plants and animals bloom and grow, because it's in their divine nature to do so.

Hu-man was created though, with the gift of free will to do in general what-ever they please. Humans were also given a gift they often overlook until it is pointed out to them, which is the power of speech, the power to communi-cate and say the word. Other creatures are not able to express in word form. If we consider the ancient stories of how the world was created with a word, what power do you think exists in this form of communication? How impor-tant are your words and what do you create with them?

I explain to my students that words do not die. As with all energy, nothing dies, it just changes form. I ask them to picture their home for a moment. Once they have the image of their home in mind, I ask them to think about what conversations (words) have been said in their home in the past year. I explain that words have a sticky substance to them. They attach themselves to people, places and things. I ask them to look at the walls and imagine they are holding up a blue light, similar to what is used to view certain stains which can not be seen with the naked eye. As they shine this blue light on their walls, they can see every word spoken in their home. All of these words are stuck on the walls, like wallpaper and they have energy in each of them. I then ask, What kind of energy have you created in your home?

Should you try this visual practice and find that you do not like the wallpaper you have created, there are four steps you can do to change the energy.

How to Consciously Change the Energy in Your Home

First, become aware of your words and how you use them, especially in your home. Where you and your family live should be the most peaceful place in your world.

Second, begin to speak more loving words of peace, encouragement, love, kindness and compassion. When engaged in an argument, catch yourself. What are you about to release energetically around you, into your home and towards the people you love?

Third, have a ceremonial cleansing ritual in your home, using white sage to smudge and cleanse the home (check with your local metaphysical store to obtain instructions on how to properly use white sage). Make sure to do the White Light prayer and cleanse yourself first in the shower, before you begin to cleanse your home. If your home has been privy to more intense negative emotions, deeds and words by you, someone else in your family or previous occupants, you may need to repeat this ritual several times. You may wish to couple this ceremony with the phases of the moon or during an equinox or solstice. It is also helpful to open all of the windows during this procedure to send the energy back out to be dispersed. I encourage all students to do this ritual at the very least, twice a year, during the Fall and Spring Equinox, in conjunction with the Spring and Fall cleaning of their home.

Fourth, is to repaint the walls in your home. Choose an entirely different color for your walls and ask for guidance to choose the color which is most needed in this room. Cleanse the room and put on beautiful, inspiring music while painting. As you begin to paint, take a section of the wall and say the word aloud that you would like the room to vibrate with, perhaps it is love, or peace or grace. With your paintbrush, lightly paint the word on the wall, while saying it out loud. Be sure to quickly roll paint over the word before it dries, otherwise you will see what you have written as it will bleed through when the paint dries.

When you are doing work of this nature, the student is always reminded that other people may not feel as comfortable with these concepts. You should not attempt to impress these teachings upon them in any way. The most important thing to remember is that one is never to interfere with another's free will. No one can know the complete destiny of another person, including what incarnation their soul is facing in this lifetime. It is pure ego that thinks they know what is best for another or what would best help another. The Neophyte student is always reminded that there is more than enough work to be done on oneself to keep busy for an entire lifetime. There is no time to be focused on what another may or may not be doing correctly. I also remind students that the best way to encourage another person is by being the best person they can be. People will notice the changes within the student for the positive. In this way, if the person wishes to speak to the student about what they're doing, the student can explain it from this perspective, rather than coming from a forceful place.

As understood by the Neophyte student by this point, there is a plethora of knowledge to be absorbed. Many attempt to do this by reading as many books and studying as many courses that they can. By doing this, they can absorb a great amount of knowledge, but until that knowledge is applied and used accurately on a daily basis, it cannot evolve from knowledge into wisdom. The gap between knowledge and wisdom in humanity can be viewed at times to be as large as the Grand Canyon.

Transforming knowledge into wisdom is when the Neophyte prepares to become an Initiate. They understand that the gulf between knowledge and wisdom is vast. At this level, the lessons move further inward toward the soul. There is less focus on acquiring knowledge and more time spent obtaining wisdom to proceed further into the mysteries. In this stage, the esoteric teachings evolve into wisdom teachings. As we see in the teachings, the lessons continue to circle back around. The questions remain the same, however, as the student evolves, so do their answers to the question. Again, they are asked:

Who Am I and Why Am I Here?

"I am part of the sun as my eye is part of me,
That I am part of the earth my feet know perfectly,
and my blood is part of the sea...
There is nothing of me that is alone and absolute, except my mind,
and we shall find that the mind has no existence by itself,
it is only the glitter of the sun on the surface of the waters."
-- D.H. Lawrence --

One example of the lessons at this level is that the student goes from understanding the concept that all is one and all is sacred, to living this concept. To live in this way is to be in balance, understanding the Divine nature of the world from moment to moment. Many monasteries teach this concept by having their monks find the sacredness in every action they do, from sweeping the floor, to cleaning, standing, and breathing. Each encounter, no matter how humble, has sacred meaning. What was once described as ordinary becomes extraordinary. This is an example of knowledge becoming wisdom.

We do not fail to be amused that the title of this chapter is called We Are Greater Than We Remember Ourselves to Be, yet in the teachings we have expressed here, we offer suggestions including finding the sacred in the most mundane, ordinary experience you can create. Indeed, it is the irony of these situations where the most valuable nuggets of wisdom are located. Such is the way of esoteric wisdom, where students are continuously pushed to see if they can see the wisdom beneath the surface.

During this period of transition, the Neophyte finds that part of who they used to identify themselves as, is disappearing or dissolving. This is the beginning of what is referred to as a death process. It is not a physical death, but rather a symbolic death of the ego and lower self. The student has begun to realize that the ego and the lower self, which they once believed was their center of power and control, is now becoming repulsive to them energetically. They can scarcely remember why they thought it was a good idea at the time to live with such control and fear. The freedom they now experience, combined with the renewal of energy and communication with the higher self, is of such great delight, that they know they are changing from the inside out. The student finds that it becomes more difficult to imagine going back to this place again. They continue to work to release old fears and work through the ego on their path to becoming an Initiate.

On a soul level, once this has been fully achieved, the Initiate lives in this place daily and connects through the heart chakra. Through a spiritual initiation, the soul is altered on many levels as are all of the bodies. At this point, one remembers who they are and why they are here.

To help all who read this book, to remember who they are and where they came from, I'd like to share an esoteric story I teach to my students. Remember esoteric stories are created layer upon layer and are multi-dimensional. Enjoy the story and see if you can see the layers within and what is being described here in this story....

> In the beginning, as with all stories, there was a Great Mother, a Queen who loved with abandon. She was pure, strong and vibrant and her greatest joys came from the abundance she produced, which happened frequently and naturally, wherever her gaze lingered but for a moment. She was indescribable, her beauty so iridescent and incandescent that to simply be in her presence transformed others. Her words spoke with such great truth and enlightenment that one was forever changed, with even a brief encounter.

One day, this Queen of the Stars fell in love. The one, who struck her fancy, was a Great Father, a King, who was as wise as he was patient, a true benevolent leader. Their love and passion were felt so strongly throughout many universes, that it continues to be spoken of to this day and has become legendary throughout the galaxies. No couple had formed a more perfect union, no love had been labeled as so Divine, both had met each other in a dance of true passion, depth and wisdom, each giving to the other in complete understanding and joy.

During this time, in this spring season of their love, while they were honeymooning in the Pleiades, they created a child unlike any that had been thought of before. This child created so much stir throughout the universes that travelers journeyed far and wide to behold her spectacular birth. She is a magnificent creation, a true balance of talent and gifts from both mother and father as she was created with a love so strong, that she positively shines with this energy for all who view her. She is known as the pearl of the sea, and is the most unique child ever created. She is capable of nestling children in her breast and restoring their energy. She has an unending supply of resources and her love for all is only matched by her beauty, generosity and willingness to forgive.

She is the epitome of every woman; strong, beautiful, opinionated, loving, yielding, and delicate. She is emotional, capable of great joy and of great sorrow. Kind and generous, and full of surprises, she is both soft and mind blowing when she speaks. She can laugh like a child, make passionate love, weep like a mother, dance like a priestess and impart the wisdom of the ages with her actions and creative energy. She facilitates the cycles of life and death, and understands why one must create and why one must destroy. She can heal with a whisper and bring men to their knees in one breath.

She is known by many titles, including: Mother Earth, the Virgin, the Mother, the Crone, Mother Nature, Queen of Heaven, Queen of the Stars, and Lady of the Moon and Stars. In ancient times, she was spoken of by many names, all in love and in respect for her. In more recent times, she has been misunderstood, misquoted and downright disrespected.

She is a wise woman, who has loved humanity through the good times and the bad, but she grows weary of what is occurring in the hearts and minds of many of the people. She has awakened from her long slumber and is ready to patiently share her wisdom again, in the hopes it will inspire others to reconnect and rediscover the ancient wisdoms as well as to help each of us remember the truth which lives within our hearts and souls.

In doing so, she has put out a call… to all those who have eyes to see and ears in which to hear. She has awakened, she is dancing once more and she invites all who have protected and kept her magic, to heed her call and gather once again in her name. She also invites all of humanity, young and old, to celebrate again, to rediscover the balance and wonder of the Divine Feminine. The shift is happening, even as these words are read, the journey has begun.

Her name is Gaia and these are her teachings.

The Teachings of Gaia – Speak to the Queen

> *"In every woman there is a Queen.*
> *Speak to the Queen and the Queen will answer."*
> *-- Norwegian Proverb --*

For too long, the world has been out of balance, dominated by the masculine energy. The universe and the earth work at their highest and best when there is equal balance between the masculine and the feminine. Many ask, where has the feminine energy gone? The answer is, it has always been here on Earth and always will exist in one form or another.

What has occurred however is that humanity, through troubling times, has pushed that energy away and at times sought to destroy it. They do not understand that nothing can truly be destroyed, for energy remains forever. Its form can alter, just as water can take many forms, including the ability to freeze, flow or evaporate. Yet even in the process of evaporation, it still exists, in another form, until it recreates itself again. The same can be said of the Divine Feminine, like her parents, she is a loving and patient being of light. Her parents created her with love and free will to proceed as she was led and she in turn, offers these same gifts to the children of Earth. Like any mother though, she can love the child, while not approving of their actions. She has been loving and protective of her children as they were growing up and held her tongue during the difficult adolescent years. Now, we have become young adults and the time for us to take and not give back has ended. The circle of life needs to be restored and replenished so that all can continue to flourish and grow. As with all children, there is a time to metaphorically leave the nest, where each person accepts responsibility and understands the accountability for each action that is taken. This is that time. We are not without assistance, she offers all of her wisdom teachings for us to use and she is always waiting in the wings, answering our call and ready to guide us when we are ready.

To begin, look for the clues she has left around the Earth. They are hidden from the masses who are too busy to pay attention to such things, yet they exist in plain sight. They are in nature, in caves, in art, sculpture, and ancient architecture, in the seasons, in the moon, in the gardens and in the seas. Hear her whisper in the wind, follow her dreams by the light of the moon and a gift from the sea will produce your first clue.

To speak to the Queen, find somewhere peaceful to spend some time, by any type of running water is always helpful. Quiet your mind, and release any negative emotions you have been carrying inside of you. She understands that many of your feelings have been created by experiences which caused you great pain and suffering. She also understands that holding on to this energy can not help you; it will only create further suffering. The path you seek is through love, wisdom and compassion, and she teaches nothing that she herself has not undergone, experienced and transcended.

She asks you to take three deep breaths. Inhale, go deep, into the fullness of your belly and then exhale fully, releasing the old stagnant energy. After three breaths, begin a new series of three deep breaths. This time inhale and feel the white light around you and bring it in through your crown chakra (at the top of your head) and allow it to circle all around and within you. As you exhale, feel the sense of lightness and energy. You feel better with this simple act of release. Once you feel this sensation, you are ready to begin your discussion with the Divine Feminine. Close your eyes and ask her to make her presence known.

Depending upon your energy, she will choose a way which is right for you at that time. It will also depend on if you are able to clear your mind and just allow it to be. She may appear to you during this time, if you are ready, or she may come in the form of a thought, inspiration or perhaps warm loving sensation which flows around you. Spend as much time as you are comfortable in this moment. When you are ready, open your eyes and look around. You may find she is with you in other ways, using nature to leave you a gift nearby. Perhaps a bird or butterfly is close, or a breeze caresses your face, or you sense her presence all around you.

You can begin to speak with her in this way and continue to reconnect with her over time. Many find that creating a sacred space in their home is a good way to continue this connection, especially to do so in the evening with the light of the moon.

Should you choose to follow the path to the inner journeys and enter a temple of esoteric teachings to become further engaged with her, you will be asked to do far greater in her service. The teachings of the Divine Feminine involve a journey of wisdom, exploration and release. In this sacred space, no one rules you, yet you are willingly in the service of the Divine.

Wherever your journey leads you, she reminds you that it will unfold as it should. Always remember to ask for your Highest and Best in all things. The Divine Feminine is of the Earth and of the Stars and the clearest way to reach her, is through the light of love and enlightened wisdom.

We hope you enjoyed this story. What may surprise you dear student, is that those who followed these teachings in ancient times, understood the balance in nature and in life and both men and women followed these teachings. Neither male or female energy is at its best on its own. What should be sought is to achieve a balance of both, which we are taught in nature, with the cycle of seasons, the balance of night and day, and the energy of yin and yang. The Universe wishes for us to embrace both to achieve balance and enlightenment.

The key to achieving the lesson of Remembering That You are Greater Than You Remember Yourself To Be, is to first connect with the energy within oneself and truly discover what one wants. The next step is to express it outwardly in open, honest communication. The conversation should focus on what is going on inside of each person, including their feelings and thoughts.

What is gained by having this conversation? The gifts are many, including renewed self-confidence, more energy and enhanced self-awareness. It also tremendously increases the chances that your relationships will be based on honesty. Your act of gentle, forthright communication opens the door for others to express themselves, without fear of the other person rejecting them or their thoughts. As this self-confidence grows within the student, the opportunity increases that they will have a clear picture of what they want and expect from life. They then are able to proceed confidently in making the changes to obtain these results.

In time, as the Neophyte practices the art of moving forward to achieve what they wish for, each student will find that their intuition is the best guide on this journey. Intuition will guide the student as to what situations they should speak out and act upon and which are best to let unfold for the experience which is occurring. The students will uncover more teachings of discernment, including a gentle knowing of when the time is right and when it isn't. The wisdom begins to unfold around them, showing them the connection to all things. It also begins to explain that they have a unique purpose in being here and that they belong in this universe.

As these teachings progress, we find that many of our greatest lessons appear to us when our minds remain open and accepting of change. The student understands there is a higher power and this force works in mysterious ways. They have the choice to listen and learn what it teaches or to turn away and thump along angrily, bumping their heads through one lesson to the next.

When a Neophyte's mind is open and confident, they understand there is no harm in expressing the fact that they are ready for more knowledge. There is nothing wrong with admitting that one does not have knowledge of all facts. They know they can say, "I don't know" and ask for the subject matter to be further explained.

The student is aware of the power of changing one's mind when information is presented which feels right to them. By the time they are aware of these powers, the student has grown tremendously in their work. The mind is clear and strong and emotions have less sway over decisions. This does not mean they are without emotion, in fact, their emotions are stronger and have more clarity of reason and purpose. Gone are the airs of deception, conniving and manipulation.

The Neophyte has gained the ability to express themselves fully in their relationships. They have discovered through the law of attraction that people are more accepting and responsive to their ideas. Perhaps even more surprisingly, they are respected more for their newly-gained strength and straight forward communications. In this comes true power, and with true power, one loses a never welcome guest, called fear.

When connected with one's power, fear has no room to live. This opens up many new doors and opportunities. Gone is the feeling and worry of rejection or concern of what someone will think of them. This frees the student to make mistakes, to try new things, all without feeling bad, or being labeled as a failure. Instead, the wise student knows they are only truly living if they are making mistakes along the way. Only the foolish, (those who remain stuck in their limited minds and stringent belief systems) are making mistakes in life. The mistake is being too wrapped in fear. Fear paralyzes them, so that they refuse to try new things. Their life is controlled through delusion, calculations of perceived risks, failures, and embarrassments versus rewards. In this mindset, they are lost in a spell of entrapment around themselves which they continue to feed daily. This fear leads to anger, though they do not realize they are doing the harm to themselves.

The Neophyte student realizes that sometimes the most logical thing to do in a situation is to act illogically, with abandon and joy. They understand that this process can lead to the most magical and enchanted of all situations and answers in life. They learn to dance with abandon, throwing their head back to laugh with the moon, swing amongst the stars and be embraced by the earth. The student knows the feeling of truly being alive and that they are a magical child of the universe. They are aware that they choose the course of their life and they do so with complete understanding, reverence and acceptance of the changes and consequences which come with each choice they make.

Rather than fearing what will come next, they welcome it, knowing that with discernment and an open heart and mind, they will learn from each experience and grow. The Neophyte also trusts in the fact that there are special people who enter their lives each day. They have only to ask for help from their guides to understand the lessons at work in their daily lives and experiences.

Now that you've been given this gift by the ones who came before you, take this lifetime and make it your own. You alone have the divine right and gift of your life.

Do You Remember Who You Are?

Chapter Seven

Lesson Six:
We Know That Only The Good Is Real

> *"Learn to get in touch with the silence within yourself,*
> *and know that everything in this life has purpose.*
> *There are no mistakes, no coincidences.*
> *All events are blessings given to us to learn from."*
> *-- Elizabeth Kubler-Ross --*

We are all One, One Energy from One Light, and as such, We are all Beings of Light. This means at the end of the day, we are all connected. The only difference between one of us and another is how far we have moved away from this light which exists within us.

To understand this, let's use the analogy of how we view our world through our perceptions. Imagine this is your first day on earth. You are an adult and have just been dropped off in the desert at 6 a.m. You are greeted by a beautiful sunrise, birds are singing, and as you walk about, the sand is warm beneath your feet. Your first day on earth is enchanting, flowers bloom on a cactus, creatures move about sunning themselves on rocks and you feel a connection with everything around you as you journey through the desert. As the day progresses, the effect of the moment wears off and as you continue to wander, you begin to have experiences you would define as less than desirable. Pests begin to buzz around and bite you on the neck and legs. You grow weary, thirsty and hungry, and while the surroundings are warm, there is no space available where you can rest. You call out for help. The sun continues to shine, the breeze continues to blow, but there is no assistance you can find. As you continue walking through the desert, you seek the shelter of a rock overhang, only to find that it is inhabited by other creatures who do not welcome you and you are quickly chased away. You feel anxious and abandoned. Fear creeps further into your mind, created by the experiences you are having and you feel less connected to the earth. At dusk, the sun sets, and you feel even further disconnected. You are cold and alone and can no longer see what is coming towards or around you. You wonder where do you go, what do you do? The world once seen as magical and entertaining has quickly changed to a place of real concern, where anything could happen to you at anytime.

After spending an exhausting and frightening night alone, the sun rises the next morning, but this offers you no solace today. It only serves to shed light on the situation that you are tired, hungry, and thirsty and not sure where to go next. It appears that hidden dangers are around you with each step you take. It becomes difficult to remember that you chose this journey and were excited to leave home and embark upon this adventure. You begin to wish that you were a child again, with your mother and father, who took care of everything and you had no decisions to make.

This scenario is comparable to what is experienced in a lifetime whether it begins when a child goes to school and is rejected by their peers on the playground, or when working for a small wage unable to make ends meet. Hundreds of stresses and strains surround each of us everyday, including the demands and struggles of relationships, including relatives, dating and marriage, raising children and maintaining friendships. There is also the time consuming attention of holding down a job, embracing a career, and caretaking of the elderly or infirm; combined with interpersonal struggles of feelings of unworthiness, self-esteem insecurities and the feeling of no time. If this is not enough, there are fears of harm happening to self and loved ones. These can be as simple as driving in heavy traffic with concern for an accident, to illness, and dangers while a child is away in school. Add political and socioeconomic worldly concerns as reported on the evening news and each person is filled with a lot of information to cause great concern.

The steady stream of fears begin in childhood, first with the realization that mother and father can not protect you from everything. Then comes the discovery that in most families, mother and father may not even stay in the same house together during your lifetime. There are experiences of not being loved and adored by everyone you meet as you enter school, to being warned about predators and crime. This continues all the way up through adulthood. These fears, what do they love to do? They love to multiply and build on top of each other. The more they multiply, the less they make rational sense. They are actually built on a shaky house of cards, but because the fear is so strong, one does not fully examine or analyze them, as this would only cause more fear!

Instead, one begins to build walls of protection around themselves, safe from the dangers of the world, safe from rejection, safe from risk. On this quicksand foundation, people convince themselves they are creating a wall of safety and they pile it on, brick after brick, and the wall grows higher and higher.

It happens gradually, one night you are out dancing with friends and a person comments as they walk by, "Look at that girl dancing, how ridiculous, who does she think she is?" This comment stings you and you are embarrassed. Up goes a brick, no more dancing in public which takes care of that problem, you'll never have to hear a comment like that again.

On a different day, you volunteer to organize an event for charity. While at the fundraiser, someone comments on how this event could have been better run if they were in charge. Ouch, this stings, bitten again by another pest! You go home and vent, telling your family and friends how after all that work, someone put down your idea. No matter that a hundred other people enjoyed themselves, all you heard and all that you remember is that one person spoke negatively about the event. No problem, up goes another brick, you vow to never help anyone in the future. You are safe, never to hear these comments again.

You go to work, your self-esteem is feeling low, after all, no one liked your dancing and your event planning skills are apparently lower than you had thought. Your mind is preoccupied with these thoughts and you are not as engaged as you normally are in the company meeting. After the meeting, your boss pulls you aside for a chat, he says that your performance has not been up to par lately and he is concerned. You assure him there is no problem and double up on your workload to prove it. Your first private thought is that you don't like your job and you want to start your own company or move to a job that allows you more creative expression. However, after that event planning fiasco, it's evident to you that you have no business starting a business and certainly, no other company would have you, so the fear doubles now that you could lose your job and lose everything you've worked for. If this happened, what would you do, where would you go, you feel lost and alone. How did you get here anyway? You miss home, you are wandering in the desert, fighting off the pests, with nowhere to rest.

Both of these examples speak of the same journey, which is a journey in which we wear ourselves down with a negative experience and allow fear to become our master. When we live in fear, we lose all sense of logic and reason and we can not think intelligently. We are too consumed with putting up bricks around us, concerned only for ourselves and keeping safe from emotional pain, physical pain, and judgments from others, which creates mental anguish. We are living in the dark, having built such encompassing walls of fear, that we have effectively blocked the light and it can not be easily felt, which is why it feels so far away and disconnected.

The worst part is, when we are in this situation, we actually think we have done something wonderful. We believe we have effectively created a safe place, a haven. This is one of the most difficult lessons to help a Neophyte student step through, as they must see for themselves how absolutely miserable they are living in this place. Then if they are ready and have the eyes in which to see, it becomes apparent to them that they have not built a safe haven, but rather a prison around themselves which keeps the world and everyone and everything in it away. They begin to see that they have imprisoned themselves from all of the beauty and joy which exists in the world. They are living at best, a half life, in the shadows, fearful and afraid.

In this self-imposed prison, they watch from the shadows, resenting the others who move about in the light, smiling and laughing, so at ease with no fear. In their anger, they build upon their delusion, convincing themselves they are better people, and that these other people must not be nice people. They must do something terribly wrong to live this way. They are confused, wondering why others don't agree with their ideas. They think to themselves, my walls are such a good idea, why haven't these other people built these walls? Why don't people tell them horrible things about what they do? Look at that girl, she's not so wonderful, her idea isn't that great, why is she coming around again to do it again, who does she think she is? And look, someone is patting her back, telling her she did a good job, how unfair. I am here at work, working longer hours than most everyone at the company and she takes a long lunch every Thursday, how unfair! There is a great breakthrough lesson to be had here dear student, for one of the biggest stumbling blocks a student has in this mindset, is their expectation that everything must be fair. There is no universal law which states that all must be fair.

Those who choose to live in the shadows can not see the world clearly. They are looking through a grey haze of fear and apprehension. As that continues to fester over time; it leads to either passive aggressive tendencies of depression, anxiety, resentment, and repressed anger or active aggressive tendencies of violence, crime, entitlement and rage. All of these only serve to move the person further away from the light.

So by now you are most undoubtedly wondering, how does this lesson even come close to explaining the concept that, Only the Good Is Real.

The secret to understanding this concept is:

> Fear may appear to be real, but it is not.
> It is a series of perceptions,
> based on experiences
> which have created an emotion.

It is your choice to feel any emotion you wish. However, you must understand, that no one can make you feel any emotion, without your consent to do so. No one can make you cry or make you laugh or make you happy. You choose your feelings about any situation.

This alone is an enormous esoteric teaching. Once you realize, that you are in control of how you choose to feel, you begin to understand that you can choose to not live in fear or doubt ever again. This begins with understanding that fear, is an instinct created to help us stay alive and survive. It is useful in certain situations. For example, if you are near a volcano and hear rumbling, fear may tell you to run, and you do so, thereby escaping being in the path of hot lava.

However, logic or intuition, could have told you to do the same thing and you would have moved equally as well, at a more calm level. In most cases, fear is an unnecessary and inhibiting factor in daily life. So when you don't speak up at a meeting where something is happening that you are really against, and you allow it to happen without speaking your mind, you have let fear win again. All because of when you spoke up in the seventh grade and someone made a snide comment about what you said. Here you are, a grown adult, years later, giving away all of your power to someone in middle school who isn't even aware of what happened in that moment. I ask you, "How many times a day do you give your power away to others, on the fear of what they might think, what they might say, or how they might judge you?"

At this point of the lesson, I share two upsetting bits of information with my students which are:

a.   When you live in fear, you are living life as a selfish, self-absorbed person. This concept is so difficult for people to take in at first, especially for women. They will disagree and say, "How could you say that, I fear for my children, to keep them safe." This is obviously a long lesson to unravel and unwind and clearly it could take an entire book to explain the complexities of this teaching. For the purpose of this book and general overview, we will simply say that we understand that parents love and care for their children and do their best to ensure their wellbeing and safety. What we are attempting to explain is that there is a very large difference between living in fear and control versus working as a parent to teach a child how to be safe. Positive ways to do this include educating a child on how to handle themselves in situations, by allowing them to learn and grow and make decisions each year as they evolve. In this direction, they become stronger, more capable and develop problem solving skills which they take with them into adulthood.

Living in fear for a child, does not teach these skills. When a parent lives in fear, they seek to control. They decide to teach the child by making most of the decisions for them, based on their own set of fears and often times selfishly, by not wishing to have to deal with situations. Think on this and see if you can recall an example of this type of situation, which was either done to you as a child or which you have done out of fear in some way to yourself or another. As we said, this is a tiny example, given the time and space afforded in this introductory teachings book. We are not attempting to discuss the complexities of child psychology or parenting, this is just used as an example of how fear can affect a situation.

> *"Parents can only give good advice or put one on the right paths,*
> *but the final forming of a person's character lies in their own hands."*
> *-- Anne Frank --*

The second part, which is equally unpleasant to hear, is:

b.   When you live in fear, you are not as interesting as you think you are. People may comment on you for a moment, but you are quickly forgotten as they move to more interesting subjects in their lives. They do not spend days, weeks, months and years agonizing and gossiping about you as you think they do.

When one lives in fear, a debilitating side effect occurs. Because the person has built so many walls and blocks, it is difficult to let feelings, emotions and love in to the person. As a result, the person feels isolated and becomes increasingly disconnected with the world. This in turn, affects their auric field and creates a murky or spongy mist around them which keeps them from feeling the light as discussed earlier in this chapter.

Because the person is not fully engaged in life, they are left with little interaction but their fears, so everything is heightened and at times blown further out of proportion. A trip to the store, where the person experiences an irritated glance from someone shopping at the store, sparks a series of emotions that bothers the person not just in the store, but even when they are back in their home. It proceeds further. Simple events such as having to engage in conversation with a neighbor or person whom they do not know very well brings a series of challenges and anxiety, and the person begins to close themselves off further and further.

As the person closes off to society, they spend more time away from people and emerge only when necessary including going to work or to perform other family duties. Because they are clouded by fear in this area as well, they view people as untrustworthy and they create stronger walls. With so many walls disconnecting them from their feelings, they lose compassion and the ability to love openly. In every aspect of the word, as we have touched on previously, they harden. In work scenarios, people are seen as a means to an end, and the energy is spent to get that person to do what they need them to do, whether its to manipulate them into buying their product or service, or do what they need done within their corporate position.

In fear, there is never enough. You have to constantly worry about money. You could lose money, or your job. In this mindset, people are viewed as constantly trying to take your money, seeing you as an easy mark. Everyone can see that you did not get the best deal, you failed again. They saw through you and made a fool of you. You'll never have enough, everything is so expensive, the world is a frightening, cold, dark place, and you must fight to make your money. If you hurt a few people in the process, it's just the way it goes; you were only doing it to take care of your family right? Besides they probably deserved it, right? There's no one as good as you in the world, which is why you had to build all those walls. If only everyone would understand that. Why don't they understand?

As a teacher, I know that these scenarios are difficult to hear because for many they will anger and touch you at a personal core level. You recognize yourself in part of these examples and want to defend yourself and your actions. You wish to educate and explain that it is a tough world and that what you are doing, is what everyone else does to survive.

But I'm here to tell you that these things are not universal truths. I'm here to wake up your mind and make you think! There are other ways to live and many people are walking these paths and never looking back. All that it takes is being willing to remove the shackles of fear and step back into the light. It does not mean that everything you've ever desired falls willingly at your feet. But, it does mean that you're back in the land of the living, back in the game, living in love and abundance and joy. From here, anything is possible, where as in fear, nothing seems possible.

Wouldn't it be nice to live in peace? Imagine living where you didn't have to work to keep those walls up all day long. A place where you didn't feel that you had to step on someone every day or talk someone into doing something you don't feel good about. No longer would you have to pretend that these things don't bother you, ignoring the physical signs when you go home at night with a headache or an upset stomach or bowels as the guilt churns away inside of you. Wouldn't it be nice to explore living in love, allowing the universe to unfold as it will? How about embracing the sacred act of asking for highest and best, knowing that with each experience, you are moving closer to awakening to all of the possibilities which exist in the world?

Once a student takes in this knowledge, they can see that action is the next step. A person can not release fear, without stepping into action and creating a completely different action, which causes the effect of an equally enhancing reaction!

This leads us to the greater lesson, where applied knowledge becomes wisdom by understanding that: All that Happens, Happens for Good. This does not mean that everything that happens "feels good" or that you will perceive it as good. It means: All that happens, regardless of how you choose to feel about it, is happening for the greater good. This experience comes in many forms to teach you a lesson which helps you grow on your path. It may also be sent to motivate or prod you forward to another experience, or impress upon you how you need to shift into new thinking. It can also serve as a mirror to reflect what is going on in your life or clear up a bit of karma from this life or another. The difference is that you are no longer bound by fear, so you can free up all of this energy to look objectively at each experience. This allows you to explore whether you have something to learn from this experience, and determine why these things are happening to you. If you do not care for these experiences, including why you continue to attract a certain kind of person into your life over and over again, ask yourself, what is the universe trying to teach you?

You will have a great amount of catching up to do here, as you have been busy building walls and ignoring your soul for years. When your walls begin to come down, you will need to remind yourself that others have been working hard to continue to push ahead, facing their fears, falling down and getting back up again. Do not resent their progress, rather see it as a goal to work towards. In order to move forward, you must greet every day as an opportunity to learn something new about yourself and others. Understand it to be an opportunity to work on yourself and grow, to help not only you, but others as well.

Remember it takes time to become the person you've always wanted to be.

Students are asked to find the ability to laugh at themselves, to persevere through challenging times and find the courage to stand strong and face situations head on. Because we feel the same fears, there aren't people out there who do this easier than others. The only difference is that they choose not to be controlled by their fear. They choose life and happiness. They know that no matter what difficult decision they face, they will get over it and can laugh and grow from the experience. They discover the greater good within themselves and others and understand that this perceived dark moment will pass and something better is coming around the corner. The biggest difference between living this way versus living in fear is understanding that regardless of the experiences you have had in the past, regardless of how you were raised, what your parents did, and what happened to you, you are not a sum of your past. You are a product of the Now and what you choose to be today. Previous experiences may have affected you, slowed you down and created blocks, but they are put aside in order to live the life that you have always wanted to live.

In the teachings, students ask, how will I overcome my fears? You make it sound so easy, but it is not that easy to do. My fears keep me safe, they are real and these things really do happen, I can show you! To answer them, I reply, Yes, they can happen, anything can happen, but this does not matter. What does matter is how you face these experiences. There is no simple step by step guide of how to face your fear; it is as complex and unique as is each individual. I can not describe exactly how it occurs for each person, but I can describe when it occurs, which is when a person has had enough… when they are so exhausted from trying to keep it together, and things still fall apart. They reach a point, where the soul cries out and says No More; I cannot continue to live like this. I am unhappy and I don't understand why and nothing seems to work anymore. When the soul reaches this point, the person dangles on a life-altering precipice of decision. At this crucial point, they can choose to go further into the darkness, leading to additional self-made delusions of control through dominance, avoidance and anger. Or the person chooses to open further, at which point an awakening occurs. When this happens, the mind has the realization that it has created the world in which it lives in, by the thoughts, words, deeds and actions made on a daily basis. The knowledge is clear that these thoughts created the life it is now leading and the overwhelming desire is to change those thoughts and begin a new life right away.

Once a student is fully aware of this teaching, at the deeper layers of the onion, they can create new thoughts and make immediate changes in their life. This occurs by first understanding that the only constant in life is change and therefore, it is not to be feared, but rather embraced. As the student begins to live with this knowledge; love, tolerance and acceptance quickly follow. In this energy, all is unfolding as it should according to the divine order of the universe. The student is open to whatever comes their way, understanding that each experience is presenting something new to learn about themselves, others and the universe.

The side effects to living in this frame of mind are remarkable. There is a new found zest for life and an understanding that you are in control of your thoughts and emotions. The freedom of not being controlled by others including society, family and even strangers stimulates the impulse to create and to give something back to the world. Because your thoughts are now filling you with so much love, light and joy, you have a natural desire to share this with others and be of service to humanity in some regard. You discover, as you give freely to others, it refills your cup over and over in a magical act of natural abundance.

Most people do not believe this, even when it is taught to them, even when they see others who do this, they still do not believe that it could happen for them. Fear is that strong. Fear tells them that other people are lucky or just pretending to be happy or they are foolish. They believe that these poor souls are not aware of the great dangers lurking around every corner for them and it's only a matter of time before it gets them. The urge is very powerful to live in the safety net where one feels they are right. It is a lonely world, but the urge to be safe and to avoid experience is very powerful when a person lives in fear.

At the end of the day, the individual alone has to make this decision. They must come to the understanding that it is more difficult to stay where they are, than to spread their wings and fly to unchartered lands.

When the student has reached mastery of this lesson, they have the wisdom of these two principles:

1. Only the Good Is Real

&

2. It's All Good!

Think hard on this as there is much more than what meets the eye at first glance. If one can master these two concepts, there is great wisdom and power to be obtained.

Chapter Eight

Lesson Seven:
We Recognize That We Are Children of the Universe

"Security is mostly a superstition. It does not exist in nature, nor do the children of men as a whole experience it. Avoiding danger is no safer in the long run than outright exposure. Life is either a daring adventure, or nothing."
-- Helen Keller --

Mysteries schools teach adults, however at the same time, it is the goal of the teacher to return each student back to the thoughts they held as a child, where anything and everything was possible. It is through this mindset, that the student can access the gifts given to them in each lifetime.

As children of the universe, we are granted many gifts including psychic/intuitive ability, and healing abilities. These gifts reside in each person. For some the gifts may come easier than others, as with all things. Some people have built up certain abilities over lifetimes and thus are able to access these talents again quicker than others.

The esoteric lessons delve into teaching the magic of the universe in various forms, including practical applications and rituals as well as philosophical and scientific applications. As the series of lessons are explored, the mind opens and the fears unwind which were clouding the heart, mind and soul from being able to access this information. As fears dissipate, renewed energy and power are restored and the student is able to proceed at a much quicker pace. This is where the fun truly begins!

In this stage of the teachings, the Neophyte is encouraged to enter into The Art of Play

Do you remember your dreams as a child? If you cannot at this time, then spend some time watching young children at play. How delightful it is to see that they are not caught up in who they are, rather they live moment to moment, in joy and creation.

One moment they are a King or Queen, later they are a butterfly or a bear and before nap time, they are their favorite cartoon character. As they embraced each of these characters, there was no doubt in their mind that they were this person, animal or celluloid creation. They understand the power of thought at its core level.

In the teachings, we encourage Neophytes to find an outlet in which they can play and be completely in the moment. I've been known to take students on adventures and outings to let loose and have a good time! An important lesson to grasp is not to take things too seriously. We are here to enjoy the world. Many Neophytes struggle at this lesson; one wouldn't think it would be difficult to take on a homework assignment which says: Have More Fun! However, many students find it difficult to embrace this lesson. The reasons vary including fear of being judged by their family and friends as not being a responsible person and fear of being perceived as silly, incompetent and frivolous. Other students have not considered doing something fun in so long that it has become a completely foreign concept to them and they are unsure of where to start. This leads the student into the journey of where and when they decided not to have fun anymore. Here we peel back another layer of the onion, which leads us into another wisdom teaching.

We are still those children in our hearts. The only difference between us now at the adult level is that we have allowed the opinions and comments of other people, along with perceived negative experiences, to have greater power over our thoughts. Through fear and doubt, we have replaced our original creative thoughts. Read this paragraph again and let it sink in. What have we done to ourselves?

The universe sent us here to the earth with great power and we give that power away.

This is a great secret that is not fully realized by most of humanity. If one truly understands this secret, then one has access to great power and possibilities.

Some rulers, both political and religious have used this information to affect humanity throughout the ages. They also understand that the secret to accomplishing this feat is not by a dramatic show of force, but rather completed in small stages. The battle is won over time, using repetition, like water beating on a rock until it wears down and yields. This is done in small doses, so subtle, that most people do not realize the effect it is having on them until it is too late.

If you take this concept and look around at the world, you will see it everywhere, in economics, politics, religion, education, mass marketing and so forth.

Over time, this happened to you as well. The story is different for each person, but the result is the same. Perhaps your parents felt whatever you did, that is was never quite good enough and they expressed these thoughts to you, either vocally or with an attitude.

Maybe it happened in school, where you were told each day you were not smart enough or did not follow instructions. Did you color outside of the lines? Write an essay from your heart, only to receive a poor grade due to grammar? Were you looked upon disapprovingly while you climbed the rope in gym class, because you were unable to reach the top?

The point is, it happens over time, bit by bit, a disapproving comment here, a look of disappointment and being teased or taunted by peers. It doesn't take long for feelings of inadequacy to come creeping in. Even during the act of growing older, the attention begins to wane, what was cute at four, is not approved or encouraged at the age of seven by the adults.

This lesson may continue to surprise you, or perhaps not, that an important lesson for each Neophyte student to undertake, is to rediscover the childlike qualities within themselves. These qualities include: laughing, silliness, joy, living in the moment, being creative without thought of judgment, play-acting, dressing up, and doing something because it's fun and for no other reason. We also ask them to try something new, which they have longed to try but never have, due to fear of failure or rejection.

We encourage students to rediscover the power of naps, and delight in taking a walk. To experience life as a child, it may mean having your entire world come to a complete halt because you just noticed a purple flower and have to investigate this further. It means understanding the importance of taking time to play and relishing in the sheer excitement of a new toy. It extends esoterically into a soul level; loving everyone you meet, knowing no strangers, only friends in the making.

The biggest difference between your physical childhood and returning to childlike qualities is the wisdom which comes with it. Gone are the temper tantrums and desires, rather they are replaced with the ability to see life through the eyes of a child, tempered with the actions of a more evolved sense of creation and action. The energy is playful, while the focus is on a larger scale.

Students are asked…
What did you love to do as a child?
When is the last time you did something like that?
What is holding you back from doing it again right now?

At first, these questions may seem irrelevant, but they lead the student to consider their dreams. In turn, this may explain the natural talents and abilities the soul came back with in this lifetime. It will also give clues as to what the soul came to experience and learn in this lifetime.

**As We Remember that
We are the Children of the Universe,**

**We also Remember that
We have a Legacy to Live up to Here on Earth.**

**There are Things to be Done,
Reasons Why We are Here.**

As with all of the teachings, the journey digs deeper and deeper into the ancient mysteries. Even the simplistic teaching of having fun, unravels more layers of wisdom for those who are ready to progress further. One of the most interesting changes on this path for the Neophyte, is that as they progress and have fun and let go, they explore all of the things which they only wished they could do before. Once they embrace these acts, their dreams seem to alter considerably from what the student thought they wanted out of life or what they wished for earlier.

This is because their inner work and transformation leads them from the 3rd chakra, into the 4th chakra energy. They are evolving. Previously they were only aware of the small spark of the Divine Energy in themselves and the world. They are now entering into a deeper consciousness and understanding.

When this occurs, magical and alchemical reactions occur and the student is more aware of self than they have ever imagined. In this same state, they wish to give to others and their joy comes from within.

As this pathway between the third and fourth chakra opens, the student journeys through inspirational stages.

The first experience is a burst of inspiration and creativity, leading to an expansion and wealth of ideas. A new found ability arises, which allows the student to intuitively understand the bigger picture of how the world works. This is coupled with the realization that it is not just about you the individual and how things affect you as a person. The student views the world through new eyes. As the old saying goes, everything old is new again. Students marvel at the beauty of everything around them, the delicate rose, the song of the birds, the elegance of sunrise and sunset, the power of touch, the energy of a smile. Everything and everyone is seen at their most profound level. This understanding is heightened and the student begins to realize how extraordinarily special every soul is on this earth and how precious is the gift of life.

The next stage is self-less love. This is where one learns about unconditional love, wanting happiness and love for others, not based upon what one is receiving back or gaining from the experience. The first level entered is the experience of compassion. Until a student can feel empathy for each person, they can not step into the higher forms of love. This one lesson alone can take lifetimes to achieve depending upon how willing the student is to open up to this concept. The most important point to explain to the Neophyte regarding this lesson is that:

Loving Someone at a Soul Level, Does Not Mean Loving Their Actions

There is a major difference between these two types of love and the student works with their teacher for a long period of time to fully understand this lesson. We trust that it is becoming very clear why it is so important for the student to first work through their thoughts and emotions and then through the ego, before beginning to work on this level.

The Third stage is entering into Divine Love. In this energy there is love for all beings, all energy, and all things. There is no perception of good or bad, there is only energy. The love goes to all things on Earth and extends outward from there.

As this energy builds with each stage, one begins to focus less on desires and instead they transmute into aspirations. One tends to think less about "self" and more about humanity and how their thoughts, actions and deeds affect everyone, not just if they make the individual feel good. At this stage, a person tends to think about highest and best for all involved and will take action to do things which are for the greater good.

During this time, one experiences a variety of tests and challenges. Desires you thought were most important may dissolve. Relationships will change and alter as well. This can leave you with a feeling of loneliness, combined with a sense of knowing that there is more and wanting that more as soon as possible. It then becomes apparent that what it is, is not found in material possessions, but rather is a spiritual gift on its way.

As you develop, you begin to understand that it is not really a separation, for in truth; you are more connected to humanity than ever before. What you are experiencing is your soul and its journey to connect with the Divine Energy again on an even deeper level. Thus begins the next journey…

To proceed, one must ask, what is Unconditional Love?

Unconditional love, means as it says, love without conditions. There can be great misunderstandings with this lesson and it would take an entire book to expound on this one concept. How can we mention above that Loving Someone at a Soul Level, Does Not Mean Loving Their Actions, yet we state, love unconditionally? It appears to be a paradox. This is but one of the many examples of why the teachings are taught preferably in oral fashion, from teacher to student, so that the teacher can be assured that the student fully understands the intent of the lesson. We can only begin to explain in this book, the simplest teachings on love. In answer to this paradoxical question, we can say that, Loving Unconditionally means, loving someone without trying to force them to bow to your will.

As we mentioned earlier, one of the rules an esoteric student learns is how to transform from living in lower forms of love to entering the higher realms of unconditional love. They understand that most people have been taught love only in its most basic, rudimentary and shallow forms. As a child they were told, I love you, because you're good and you do the right things. Not I love you, because of the wild and wonderful creature that you are!

So an important lesson for any aspiring Initiate to achieve is the Lesson of Unconditional Love. As you can see, this lesson can only be carried out, once one has mastered the lesson of self-awareness, otherwise one will not have the inner self-confidence and strength to live and love unconditionally.

The tools required for this lesson include not only an open heart and mind, but a great degree of unselfishness on the Neophyte's part. The lesson here works with the Heart Chakra and the Third Eye, which allows one to see the world and all of its inhabitants in a completely different light. This occurs at the Initiate level; where the student has become aware that help is always available to them from the other side. They only need to recognize it is there and ask for guidance as needed.

While we have journeyed deep into the levels of this lesson, we recognize we have left a great amount of food for thought with this teaching. For the purpose of this lesson here, we recommend that Neophytes go back and start at the beginning of this chapter, which is to have more fun. While this sounds like a most surprising direction, levity is a path to enlightenment.

Chapter Nine

Lesson Eight:
We Are Limitless and Ageless, All That Exists is Now

"Twenty years from now you will be more disappointed
by the things that you didn't do than by the ones you did do.
So throw off the bowlines. Sail away from the safe harbor.
Catch the trade winds in your sails.
Explore. Dream. Discover."
-- Mark Twain --

To fully explore this concept, students are asked to remove their predisposed conclusions about living in a three dimensional world and instead to explore the possibility that they can and do access fifth and sixth dimensions from various planes. Once this idea takes root in the mind and is considered to be conceivable, amazing experiences begin to arise, both within the mind and the soul.

When the student grasps the idea that, we are limitless, ageless and part of the infinite, the idea of time as we know it on this third dimension becomes less interesting. The student begins to see that in this world, they do not move through time, but rather, time moves through them. They are all that they have been or will be, in many ways.

As we begin to teach the students these concepts, they build one on top of the other and the mind and soul take flight. It is a bit like the old television show, where Mr. Rourke would say, "Welcome to Fantasy Island." One begins to realize that anything and everything is possible, if willing to put enough thought and action into achieving a goal or dream. It might not happen overnight, but it can and will happen if the focus remains.

What does this feel like, to finally realize that you are ageless and there are no limits to the possibilities? That while your physical body may stop working in this lifetime, you will continue on. Your body will be replaced and possibly even upgraded, with a new vehicle for you to move around in when you return back to the earth plane. And that even during the time when you are not on this plane, you remain and live and thrive.

Physicists are hinting about discoveries of the fifth, sixth, seventh, and up to even the eleventh dimension. Science is exploring areas that mystics have taught for ages. All which is seen here with the naked eye is not all that exists. There are other planes, (realms of existence), where spirit lives in various forms and these other planes have laws and forces which affect where we live here on earth.

Currently, scientists are exploring other dimensions to understand how and why gravity is such a weak force on this earth. These are not merely concepts on paper. A laboratory in Europe, is creating an underground particle accelerator which may be able to produce subatomic particles in other dimensions. While the force of gravity is not the highest pressing issue for an esoteric student, the scientific information gathered while probing the concepts of these planes from this perspective, can yield valuable fruit for the mind. Esoteric teachings have always flourished when scientific and spiritual people worked together, as it was in the days of da Vinci and in ancient Egypt, Greece and Rome. During these ages of enlightenment, diverse parties shared information to expand the knowledge. Spiritual teachings were philosophies, rather than doctrine and science was willing to explore the most unconventional of concepts.

So as we turn back to this lesson, that we are ageless and limitless, this lesson is another of the most misunderstood lessons. When students hear this lesson, they say, "Well if I am all that I have ever been or ever will be, why bother, it doesn't matter." This is not the case. While this sounds like an enigma, I must endeavor to explain that- All that you have is Now and all that matters is Now. Now is all that you have! (Remember esoteric teachings are mysteries, that you have to roll around in your mind and heart and this book would be remiss if we didn't leave you with at least one puzzle to ponder and think about. Our hope is that after reading this book, that you may be inspired to study the teachings further and begin your own journey).

The consciousness of the moment where your thoughts are focused, creates what is going on around you. In this understanding, there is no future, there is only Now, which is created moment by moment.

When a student fully understands this lesson, magic occurs. It is what others call the Aha moment, a Eureka! All the lessons of the thoughts, emotions, dreams, and energy, culminate in the realization that they all can be activated Right Now! There truly is no moment like the present. The flip side of this understanding is that one can no longer talk in terms of the past and regrets of what could have been done. Nor can they express that they do not know what the future holds, for they are creating their future with every thought, word, action and deed.

This leads us to one of the greatest understandings of how only the good is real, as we discussed in a previous chapter. Thoughts, as we have discussed earlier, are formed in other planes and then come down into the physical realm, as do other forms of energy. Why is it that Only the Good is Real? The answer is because the Good (Love) is from the highest planes of existence. The other forces which we experience on the earth plane are forms which only exist on this plane and lower planes.

One of these forces is the concept of Fear. This is why Love wins over Fear. Love is a Universal Truth, a Universal Law which comes from the highest of planes. To be in its presence supersedes all other feelings. Remember here that we are talking about Love in its highest forms, not the selfish love people confuse in relationships where they wish to control or have ownership over another. In the presence of universal love, fear does not exist.

These concepts and teachings have been taught through many ages in various forms, to reach people in ways they can understand at the time. Recently, people are connecting with the energy that by being aware of their thoughts and believing they can achieve abundance, they can create and attract this energy to them. These are ancient teachings which have been taught to students who were ready to hear and work to master them.

The reason many people do not move forward in the teachings, is because they are unwilling or unable to devote the time and energy required to focus their thoughts on these new discoveries within themselves and stay with them until the changes begin to take form. It takes a certain amount of faith and determination to go through this journey and persevere. One of the most difficult experiences a student faces, is looking back at their past to understand where their beliefs, habits and fears began. As they work to reorganize these patterns, which we refer to as cleaning house, everything around them, including their thoughts, relationships and emotions often becomes messier and more complicated before they can be resolved and restructured.

This is a daunting proposition for the heartiest of souls when faced with what they may deal with as they begin to look at the repercussion of their actions. If you have read this far in the book and are even considering the possibility of wanting to study further into the esoteric teachings, you are known as part of the 2% of the people in the world who are willing to do so at any given time.

Should you continue on the journey and begin to study the path from Neophyte to Initiate, you would then become two percent of the two percent. These people are willing to look completely within themselves on the journey to awakening, while wrestling with the ego who desires to remain in control. As with anything which comes with great rewards, the journey can be perilous and daunting, and requires daring souls who are willing to open their hearts and accept some modicum of risk for reward. Perhaps this is why those who are willing to do so, also connect with the law of attraction and abundance and are willing to put themselves out there to try new ideas and take risks in this manner. They also have learned another important lesson, which is not to be attached to the outcome. This is also referred to as understanding that life is not about reaching the destination, but rather how one handles the journey.

The outcome of a situation is not most important, what happens in the in-between is what matters and how one handles what happens in the in-between. The knowledge gained in that time, produces energy and the outcome is a reflection of that energy. If one does not care for the outcome, then it is time to look at the mirror of reflection shown in this outcome and examine what thoughts were not aligned with the focus of the goal.

Once these are understood, they can be reapplied with renewed focus and clarity, in order to receive the desired outcome. Shampoo, Rinse, Repeat, it's that easy! Why this is not effective for more people is because they become too emotionally and mentally caught up in the outcome, rather than looking at it as a temporary state of being or existence, which can be altered over and over again. They are attached to the outcome as a final state, yet have we not taught that nothing in life is constant, but change, so how can any outcome be final? The absurdity of the logic begins to come forward in an entirely new light.

Most students find they can accept the teaching of living in the now. The true struggle comes in facing issues they do not wish to face within themselves. It is much easier to say that one can not accomplish something because an experience in the past is holding them back or that they must wait for the future events to change before they can proceed. To live a life of action and possibility in the now, requires that one release all doubts and fears and begin to create the life one wishes to have, with the understanding that it is all available now.

The other most surprising discovery, is how much time one spends thinking about anything and everything but what they are doing right now. Most people go through their day with no thought to their surroundings or what is happening at the moment. At work, they are worried about home, at home, they are worried about an appointment they have in a week. They are unable to shut these thoughts down and let them be. What will be, will be. Yes, perhaps there will be traffic when you leave for vacation, but will thinking about it today change that possibility? If we go deeper into peeling the onion, we could say yes, it can change that outcome, from a possibility to a certainty. The more thought you give to the idea that there will be traffic when you go on vacation, the more energy created to ensure that you will indeed attract what you are asking to come to you.

If you wonder about this teaching, notice the person in the car next to you in traffic one day, who appears to be in a terrible rush. Their car is next to yours at the red light, the difference is when the light turns green, they race their car to get ahead, darting between cars, inching up further. Yet at the next traffic light, they are sitting at the same light that you have calmly approached. Perhaps they are one car ahead of you, but at times, they may even be in the lane next to you, a car behind you, as they became stuck behind a large slow-moving vehicle. Light after light, you continue to keep pace with them, though they continue to race to beat time. When they arrive at their destination, it is not difficult to imagine their mood, energy or their thoughts about their day, because we have all done this at one time or another, not wanting to look at what these actions were doing to us.

So yes, in answer to the thought, will there be traffic on the road when I leave for vacation, the answer is probably yes. If there is a road, the likelihood of vehicles on the road is certainly possible and likely probable, but how you handle this situation, (the in-between) is what matters most. Why are you giving your precious energy and time to worrying about something that already exists? Students who are serious about the teachings, quickly see the futility in such thinking, as it only serves to cause chatter in the mind, and create negativity towards a situation which does not need to have such energy attached to it. There are so many wonderful ideas to focus on instead regarding vacation, including what beautiful sights you will see, and the fun you will have when you are there. When focusing on these thoughts, you are already creating them and sending this energy to further attract and amplify these thoughts of beauty and fun.

Now that you understand this concept, do you really wish to go back to thinking in the old ways you were used to doing? The walls are beginning to break down and the soul once imprisoned inside in the idle chatter and blocks of fear is ready to soar to new heights of experiences.

Living in the now, is a joyous moment of awakening.

Once awakened, everything changes. You notice the beauty in your surroundings, in everything you see, feel and touch. The energy in each moment, the joy of conversation with others, the brilliant forces of nature in all its glory, all is unfolded in front of you. It's as if you are seeing everyone and everything for the first time.

As we mentioned in an earlier chapter, some orders teach this to their monks by having them find the joy in every moment, whether it is sweeping the floor, cleaning a dish or working in the garden. Every action becomes sacred, an exercise of living in the moment. All is divine in its action, creation and form. Many students find that martial arts or accompaniments like meditation, yoga, tai chi or art classes help them to step out of themselves as they are working on this lesson.

The question then to ask is… How can I experience more of "whatever it is that I want" right now? When you find the answer to this question, and begin to act upon it, you are living in the moment.

Let's review notes on how to live in the Now

1. Every action is an amazing, inspiring opportunity, waiting for us to go forth with creativity, inspiration and exuberance.

2. Each day you recognize your true existence. You are fully alive and engaged in many planes of consciousness.

3. Your thoughts become focused, which can change your life in this moment.

4. Seek from the awakened heart and you will find the gifts and the answers you wish to receive. This can be accomplished through this inner soulful journey.

5. The universe recognizes you as a creative, intuitive being of light. You have all the time in the world, right now.

Perhaps no one understood this better than Anne Frank, who wrote in her diary, "*How wonderful it is that nobody need wait a single moment before starting to improve the world.*"

This leads one's thoughts again to, Who Am I? If you have considered the principles brought forth thus far in this book, it will have caused you to question this even more times than we have asked of you. You have begun to see how the esoteric teachings work, patiently repeating information, going deeper each time, prodding a bit more to encourage you to untangle the webs in your mind and explore them further.

At this point of study, the student is asked the following questions

Are you the person you thought you were?
Are you someone greater than you ever imagined?

Perhaps you are the sum of all of these things and even more than has been revealed thus far. Now that you are aware of these possibilities, what will you do with them? Surely these ancient teachings were not created just so you could discover how to purchase a few more toys in your life. Perhaps there are things that you can do to be of service to the world, in some way, large or small.

When one lives in the moment, every loving act can be a gift to the world.

With each expression of kindness, compassion, generosity, non-judgment, awareness, and positive thought, one can not help but affect the people around them by the energy which is exuded in this state of being.

In this state, acts of kindness affect others and inspire them to consider positive actions themselves. Perhaps it plants a seed of thought which grows over time. Maybe it offers hope to another that the world is not such a terrible place and that happiness is attainable. It may also spark a person to create their own random act of generosity and love.

In the mystery teachings of past and present, it was just as important that one give back as it was to study and absorb the teachings. Each student used their talents and gifts to give back to the world in some way, whether they taught at schools or centers of learning, shared ideas as a philosopher, used their creative abilities to create art, heal, design buildings, prepare beautiful and nourishing meals, weave thread, create pottery, or care for and inspire children. Whatever called to the student and allowed them to reach further into themselves to create was brought forth and thus entire communities were enhanced by having this energy shared.

If you've ever wondered what it looks like or what it would feel like to see someone who lives in this energy, look for a person who's life is full of creative activity, who takes delight in the grandest and simplest of things, and who gives as much time as possible to others. In return, the most amazing occurrences seem to happen to them, over and over. When you see this in action, it will amaze you. The energy of this person will affect you, as they are warm and loving and it appears as if they have all the time in the world for you when they are speaking with you. This person is living in the moment and once you catch a glimpse of what this feels like, it will stay in your mind and you will find yourself wanting to experience what it feels like.

To understand this from a scientific standpoint, the student is taught that the chemical and alchemical reactions occurring in this stage, begins with the energy around the heart. It then spreads into the mind and is released through the other bodies in what could be described as a big bang, or moment of en-lightenment. Esoteric teachings teach that energy rises within a person until there is a cataclysmic eruption from the soul, which creates a new person, a rebirth we shall say.

The teachings explain that as one begins the process of knowing, (gnosis), and awakening, each step takes the student further on their inward journey, which builds in momentum along the way. As it grows, the thoughts, emo-tions, words, actions and deeds evolve until a rebirth of the soul is experi-enced, which alters the person on all levels. The rebirth is just the beginning, though it has taken much work to get there, as a grand series of chemical and alchemical changes have occurred within the body, turning iron into gold.

With this "big bang," the person has expanded from a uni-verse, to a multi-verse, by creating enough energy and thought matter to form and create this new life using elemental properties and forces. This ability lies within each person. It can be a self-acting and perpetuating event when the student is taught how to proceed and unlock these mysteries of the universe. This goes without saying, that this is not a Neophyte experience.

At this point, the esoteric student realizes again, that they thought they knew something, only to learn they have even more to unravel and learn over again. This will happen over and over so the best choice a student can make is to be open to change and be at peace with what they have learned. In future les-sons, they will most likely need to unlearn more things and what is unknown to them is usually far greater than what is known. Students, who excel in the teachings, understand this lesson very well. They have learned that when ask-ing for their highest and best, that all will come forth to them in divine order, when the time is right. It will be revealed from the universe as it should be, within the way it should unfold. There is a great peace and wisdom in know-ing that all of the information in the universe is available to you.

To expand further on the chemical and alchemical reactions that occur, we must first begin with the blood, which is a chief component in this mystical and sacred process. The blood and the breath are the two most important ingredients needed to create the rebirth.

As a student evolves from Neophyte to an Initiate, the work begins on the blood. Again, I must reiterate, this is a highly complex and involved series of teachings in the ancient mysteries and we can only just touch on the meaning here at this time. We can only explain in rudimentary terms here about the microcosm and macrocosm. For example, we are the microcosm of the macrocosm of our universe. If one is familiar with the understanding of a galactic center in our universe (macrocosm), then it is easy to understand that our heart is the galactic center of our body (microcosm) where energy is distributed, energized and released. Our blood is the stream of consciousness which carries the energy and the language within it throughout the universe (body). This is a natural occurrence in each person. However, when one has knowledge of esoteric wisdom and learns the language and actions which energize these streams of consciousness, (the blood) they can create an enhanced form of this energy which has both a chemical and alchemical transmutation. Intriguing isn't it?

One of the ways in which students are taught how to transmute their blood, is by understanding the great healing power which can be brought in with the breath. In our school Stella Maris, we teach that, "The Breath is The Life." Students are taught how to begin and end their day with deep breathing exercises, where they not only inhale in deeper breaths, but also pull in the energy of white light. They draw this energy into their bodies, while blowing out and releasing any negative or stale energy which has been residing inside of the body. This act, done twice a day can stimulate the body in many ways and benefit the body, mind and soul.

As deep breathing becomes a daily practice combined with conscious thought and drawing in the light, it creates a positive effect on the fields around the physical body. These two working in tandem can have amazing results! The blood stream becomes more pure as additional oxygen is coming into the body. The oxygen works throughout the body, rejuvenating it at all levels and assists with organ and glandular functions and increased vitality overall.

The breath can also help create additional energy which the body uses daily. This overflow allows for more creative and intuitive thoughts and outlets, which in return, lead the student to higher elevations of communication and action. This in turn, brings forth even higher levels of energy.

Who would think that an act as simple as conscious breathing could create such amazing results in the body, mind and spirit!

Again, as with all esoteric teachings, we always remind students not to believe these teachings, simply because we have expressed them. We encourage everyone to conduct their own research and look for this information in other sources where it is taught in other forms. Medical science speaks in various discourses on the importance of oxygen to the body, and how it sends vitality to each cell, as well as the organs, glands and especially the brain. Oxygen revitalizes the body, allowing it to restore. Yoga has shared these concepts for thousands of years. These secrets are not so secret after all. All that has been missing is the understanding behind the action and what focused intention can create.

If you have any doubt of how important the breath is, ponder this example. For one day, how you would feel if you did not eat? Now consider if you did not drink any liquid for a day. Will you make it through the day? Yes, perhaps though with some discomfort, but it can be done. Now consider not breathing. Not exactly an option is it? The breath is the life, in and out, in and out, like the ocean. The breath of the earth must ebb and flow, consistently bringing in new energy and releasing the old.

Esoteric students know that the thoughts they have and the words they speak are stored in the energy fields around the body remaining there for a long period of time. When these thoughts and words are not positive, they form a cloud around the body, which we have explained previously, acts like a screen, filtering part of the pure white light which wants to come around the body.

In this condition, when the student is trying to pull fresh air and energy into the body, it is being filtered and is not as clear. It appears murky with the heavy thoughts and emotions which are still "hanging in the air," like a "dark cloud over them." In this situation, as the student continues to breathe in this energy and bring it back inside of them, they are only receiving half of the positive energy which they could take into their body. Neophytes are asked to imagine this, to see the energy around themselves which they are creating. Later, they learn to actually see this energy as they begin working to see auras. At that point, they can see the energy around other people in this way.

As a student, once you have this knowledge, you are aware of the damage you are doing to yourself when you hold on to anger or sadness or fear. This damage is occurring in and around you, and you are breathing this energy back into your body. It becomes apparent why one should work quickly to remove and release negative energy and ask to be surrounded with the highest and best light. It is a tremendous gift to be free from negative thoughts, worries and emotions. The work accomplished in this area will pay off immediately in a multitude of ways.

Imagine what you could create in your life, even if you took no other lesson from this book, but this one: Greet each day with the deep breathing exercises and white light visualization for five minutes in the morning. In the evening, before repeating the same exercise, reflect and release any negative emotions and thoughts you had during the day. Do not allow them to stay within or around you. Release them and replace them with loving thoughts and then complete the white light visualization and breathing.

What effect do you think this could have on your body, on your heart, and your state of mind if you were to live and experience this one lesson?

In the same respect, what effect do you think occurs when one breathes in a shallow manner each day and does not release this energy?

When students master this lesson and go from Neophyte to Initiate to an

Adept, they are taught further how to work with the breath, which can allow them to travel to other dimensions through the purification and enhancement of the blood and the breath. It is a slow process because the student must work on themselves first in order to access these realms in the safest and most helpful manner for the soul.

Throughout the ages, some have sought to skip this process and experience something similar with the use of drugs, which cause altered states. This is discouraged by mystery school teachers, as it is a "false positive". When one has to rely on a substance to alter their state, it does not have the same effect on the body, mind and soul, as it does to achieve it on one's own merit and progress. It is similar to claiming to be a marathon runner, by driving to the last mile in the race and slipping out through the bushes onto the road to run the last bit of the race and claim to have won. While one may have felt a bit of the experience and the ego is certainly satisfied, there is no true connection of having prepared, worked for and successfully completed a marathon. This is because esoteric students discover that many of the secrets and the answers of the universe are found during the journey, not just felt at the destination. Beware of those offering false gifts, for they may tantalize the mind and delight the senses for a moment, but the memories will be fleeting and the knowledge gained will be brief. Rather than the delight and joy which the Adept experiences from the inside out, the journey with an altered substance leaves the person feeling further disconnected when they come down off of the substance. Their only source of reconnection is to continue to take the substance and yet, the results will diminish in time, rather than expand, as well as take its toll on body, mind and auric field. While for the Adept student, the journey nourishes them on every level and grows richer with each repeated experience.

In the age we live in now, there is no need to proceed in these ways. The ability to go within and to travel to the multi-verses is available to you now. You have but only to ask and then be willing to do the work to make the journey. The results are enormous and life-altering, not just for this lifetime, but for the ones to come. All of this hard work is stored within your personal container, the soul, which carries the wisdom you learn from lifetime to lifetime and you build upon this with each step you take into the mysteries.

To continue our alchemical discussion, the focused work on the breath clears the filters around the body. The purification of thoughts and emotions affects the bloodstream and organs, establishing a foundation which affects the physical, mental, emotional and spiritual bodies. The results create astounding changes, which are taught to Adept students. They see how the bodies refine themselves and become more pure, altering to a more crystallized form, which collects more light. This in turn creates more energy, which allows the Adepts to alter their vibrations and thus travel further and deeper into other dimensions.

As the student progresses, the body, mind and spirit continue to be affected and evolve in a myriad of ways. The energy bodies are stirred by beauty, music, creative thought and expression through language. As described in many teachings, in the beginning was the Word, (sound) and from the sound, came the light and from the light, came creation. Read this sentence over again, as it is rich with esoteric wisdom.

In addition, there are teachings which say, if you travel to the ocean and are in a state where you have opened your heart and mind, you can hear and see angelic forms which meet at sunrise and sunset at the in-between, the space where the waves meet the shore. In these moments, light beings gather to celebrate the mystical connection between the shore, the waves and the sun. This is but one of the many forms, celebrations and connections which are taught in the mystery school. Others include working with the energy of colors, understanding sacred symbols, and attuning to the natural forces and cycles of nature. Courses are presented in which students can study for a lifetime if they wish including: connections to the Divine in both heaven and earth, the esoteric science of vibrational frequencies and sound, activating chakras, clearing auric fields, and many other spiritual advancements. Some of which we have briefly touched upon throughout these chapters regarding consciousness, awakening, the energy in love, living in the moment, and working in and exploring other planes of existence. We have only begun to discuss the lessons which are available to the student who is willing to take the journey.

Chapter Ten

**Lesson Nine:
We Create the Path, Which Leads to Our Destiny**

*"What is our destiny?
To live, to laugh, to love, to be
To express ourselves in various forms
To come together, to create, to share
To fulfill that which we are to be…."
-- Kala --*

At this point, you have embarked on a journey of tremendous self-exploration and introspection. It will be clear at some level, that the culmination of these Neophyte teachings result in the understanding that each person is in control of their destiny. This journey can empower a student to live a life of their own making with renewed focus and clarity. The student also has the choice to live as they were, in a sea of emotions and random thoughts as they react from one experience to another.

To proceed further into the teachings, Neophyte students are asked to step across another line in the sand. This ritual involves accepting that knowledge of these teachings now means that they are no longer "unaware." Through the work completed thus far, the student understands they can generate greater amounts of karma to themselves by not taking action on the lessons they have learned.

The Path the student has chosen to walk on at this time is called "self-realization." It becomes evident that answers are not delivered; rather the understanding comes while exploring the journey. As Neophytes become Initiates, one lesson they have mastered is that all is revealed in the journey, not the destination. This is a difficult concept to grasp at first, especially in the western world, where almost every decision and goal, is focused on the win, the dangling carrot. It is almost inconceivable for many people to do something just for the experience, regardless of whether they win or lose. It's even more challenging to do something just for the experience, where there is no chance of winning a prize, or certificate of achievement. It appears that the journey is taken with no glory or seemingly material outcome noticeable at the time.

The next major step the student must take is to understand that two must become one. They must achieve balance within themselves, in all of their natures, combining the masculine and feminine energies. This must occur in all levels, including physical, mental, emotional and spiritual which brings forth many challenges to deal with, but also reactivates ancient knowledge of the differences between the spirit and the soul.

From this view, the path widens to as many possibilities as can be imagined. This is why we teach the concept of, "Many Paths, One Destination." All paths are honored and welcomed to be explored, as each have value and wisdom to be shared. The destination expresses the soul's desire to understand the one, where we all come from. Though we may all choose various directions on our path to exploration, we are all seeking to understand the greater mysteries and return back home as it is often described.

What paralyzes some students in their progress, is the realization that indeed one can choose any path they desire. Thus, how to choose? Will the path lead them further astray or closer to their desired outcome? Perhaps they fear what lies in the road ahead and the unknown. Students struggle with these thoughts as they seek the path and just when they think things couldn't become anymore confusing, it happens. The ego sneaks in an attack that they don't even see coming. What is this weapon of destruction? Doubt. The ego brings in its old reliable ally of fear, Doubt.

Doubt is very powerful and especially at this time, when one is unsure of how far they want to travel. Doubt brings fears back up to the surface and can cripple the strongest man if it is allowed to take hold of the mind. If a person is not truly ready to embark on their journey, doubt will give them an excuse to quit and run, using all types of fantastic excuses. The ego, (lower self), does not want to lose control. It will work to remind the person over and over that, "You have known you for a long time and things were never this hard, how can what is happening now, be good? Isn't good supposed to feel good? This experience is not feeling good."

As this battle progresses between the lower self and higher self, (ego versus soul), each student must use all of the lessons and tools which they have been taught up to this point to maintain their grip on what is happening in their life. It is common to feel isolated, as during this process, one is reconsidering the dynamics of all relationships. In addition, the student is going through the process of their thoughts and emotions being redefined and new structures are taking place on every level of the body, mind and spirit.

In the classes, I remind students to compare this experience to the dark nights of winter, when one becomes more introspective. During this time, the light appears to be far away and the cold isolates us from the warmth we love. Yet in this season, deep within us and deep within the earth, the planted seeds are being nurtured. In the depths of winter, we are only steps away the stunning beauty, birth and renewal of spring!

In this teaching, the student is reminded that as they proceed through these periods in life, the journey of attaining higher consciousness is not done in one fell swoop, but rather in cycles throughout their lifetime. The layers of the teachings unfold as the student continues to develop and expand their knowledge and understanding. It is the same with the changes of the seasons, the ebb and flow of the tides, and the cycle of the moon. This is a Law of the Universe and it all unfolds in Divine Order. As the student understands this concept, they see that even with consciousness they will not live in a state of pure bliss, where one is chanting and nothing else occurs. That is not the way of life and enlightenment today. We evolve in cycles, just like life here on earth. Spring is the time of rejuvenation and growth, Summer is the time of joy and experience, Fall is the time of harvest and abundance and Winter is the time to reflect and be reborn with new-found wisdom.

As we have stated before, the only constant in life is change. The student will not stay in one spiritual state or level of consciousness, for it is still necessary to live here on the earth plane. This includes living in the world, working, spending time with family, and expressing creatively in the many forms available in this lifetime. The goal is not to live as a monk, but to transform into a higher sense of awareness. The challenge of this new Age of Aquarius is to leave the mountain tops and caves and live in the world amongst the people. It is a wonderful achievement to live in daily life, with good intentions and a state of grace and understanding, as this energy ripples out and affects all those around you.

As the student continues on their path, they are reminded to reflect on nature as inspiration. When walking up a hill and reaching the top, there is a beautiful and peaceful valley below. This valley would not be in existence if it were not for the hills that surround it and one would not be able to experience the valley, had they not been willing to make the journey to climb up the hill. Both are equally important in the balance of nature as both have equal importance in spiritual growth.

Surprisingly, the easiest way to master this lesson is one that few students guess. It is to give abundantly and frequently to others, with no thought of reciprocation or gain. This is such a difficult concept, for in reality many times people give because they wish to procure a desired outcome. They give to another to win their favor or attention, to make themselves look better, to charm a person or receive a reaction. Even happy reasons still have expectations. When parents buy gifts for a child's birthday or holiday, they expect a certain reaction from the child. They want to feel that rush of joy. This is why Christmas is such a popular holiday; people want to feel the emotion, brought by seeing the excitement in a child or the joy in a person's face when opening a present.

Using another example, many people find it easy to give to charity, to someone who is in a worse condition or situation than they are. However, they find it difficult to give to someone to do with what they will, chase a dream, spend on a vacation or just enjoy a moment. People give with expectation, which removes the pure energy from the gift. Expectations include: how the person will react when they receive the gift, what they will do with the gift and how long they will keep and/or use the gift. There is an expectation they will express gratitude and reciprocate back to the person who gave the gift. There are so many expectations piled on with a gift that the weight is enormous and at times becomes a burden.

True giving comes with no desired outcome, expectation or thought of reciprocation. The only intent is to give to another person with joy. Exoterically, this teaching is shared in many ways including the expression, "Practice Random Gifts of Kindness." It was also portrayed in the movie, "Pay It Forward," with the understanding that one would not know what their act of kindness would do or how it would benefit another. They would simply do the act because they were able to do so and because they wanted to give abundantly. If everyone could adopt this teaching and give in this way at some level, the energy and outcomes on this world would change dramatically in a very short while.

In the esoteric classes, Neophyte students are asked a series of questions in order to see how close they are to walking their true path and following their destiny.

Here are some of the questions students are asked regarding The Laws of Abundance

1. Do you frequently give to another with no thought of reciprocation? Do you go above and beyond in some cases to give when you know that your time or talent could be of great use to a person you know?

2. Are you able and do you frequently laugh at yourself each day? Do you

enjoy the amazing occurrences and perceived struggles which are presented to you throughout your day?

3. How often do you feel love for yourself, for others, for the world, and for humanity? How often do you express this love in all of these categories in one form or another?

4. Do you take the time each day to express some of the positive thoughts you have felt throughout the day with other people?

5. Are you aware of your thoughts on a daily, even hourly basis? Do you catch yourself when you slip into a field of negative or fearful thinking you carry with you and make changes to alter the thinking and release the energy?

6. How's your breathing? Do you take the time to bring in white light and energy to take care of you throughout your day?

7. Are you living in the moment? Are you taking action on your thoughts and dreams? How often do you complain or live in the past with guilt or in the future with worry?

8. Are you awake and experiencing love, joy and abundance? Are you embracing the day?

9. Do you share and reach out to others in moments of compassion and understanding?

10. Are you connecting and taking the time each day to live in gratitude for all the wonderful gifts you are continuing to receive?

These are a few of the questions which Neophytes are asked to work on in the classes. As with all things, the further they progress, the more challenging the questions become.

Besides the act of giving with abundance, exuberance and reverence, the second act which can quickly bring your path and destiny to you, is to choose one of your life long dreams and decide to take action on this dream now, right now. There is power in making this decision and with each step taken, it grows.

One begins with the decision to bring the dream to fruition. This is accomplished first with the day-dream, (fantasizing about what one wants to achieve). Next comes a period of brain-storming, thinking about the dream and how it could be put into motion. The next step involves writing out the goals to achieve the dream. From there, it involves taking action. No matter what the dream is, there is something one can do each day to bring themselves closer to achieving the dream. Students understand the concept that taking action, even with the smallest step, awakens the dream and makes it real. This brings it from the dimension of thought, into the physical dimension. The more thought and action focused on the dream, the stronger it becomes. Taking action to create the dream is extremely powerful.

Depending upon the dream, it may not be able to be accomplished in a short span of time. However, when one speaks aloud to the universe and takes action on the dream, the universe listens. Every action has an equal reaction. This is a Universal Law and an important concept to understand and bears repeating; Every Action Has an Equal Reaction. This is not something you will turn on with the creation of your dream. This is what happens through the course of every day, with each action you take. Think on this lesson and law here carefully. Pay attention for one full day and observe your thoughts, actions, words and deeds. How did each task unfold for you throughout the day? What was your and the universe's reaction with each part? Once you are able to fully grasp this lesson, then take it a step further and positively focus on how your thoughts affect your actions, which bring forth results.

There is a lesson however, that all students must strive to show mastery before we teach them to work further on any other lesson. This teaching proves to be most useful in all aspects of life, including working on dreams and goals, working with others and making daily decisions. If this lesson is not mastered, dreams and relationships will be undermined as these battles will rise up against them in the mind over and over again. We have touched on this lesson in earlier chapters. Now we shall pull back the layers of the onion deeper, delving into the lesson of:

Understanding the difference between Judgment and Discernment

In the esoteric teachings, there is a lesson known as becoming aware of the motive behind the motive. As you awaken on your soul journey, a large part of this process includes the realization of moving out of the traps of ego and into a greater sense of understanding the grand design of the universe. In this process, an important lesson we learn is to recognize and then let go of negative attitudes such as manipulation and being judgmental or critical. We begin to think much deeper into questions such as Who Am I and what has made and molded us into the person we see before us today.

As we delve further into our consciousness, we must let down the walls of defense we created to protect ourselves from being hurt. This is the scariest moment, as it requires moving from fear into the unknown destiny. Many times, we do not realize we were operating from such a deep place of fear in parts of our lives. This in itself is a tremendous awakening.

As we let down these walls, we begin to see that the judgment of ourselves and others are based on our fears. We can understand this by looking at the purest of people, children. When we hold a baby, it seeks only to feel safe and loved and to have its earthly needs met, a warm blanket, a full stomach, what are known as creature comforts. As the baby becomes a child, it begins to learn fear. Perhaps the people on whom the baby relies on the most, startle the baby one day by raising their voice in anger and frustration and the loud sounds and energy vibration scare the infant. Even at this stage, the baby begins to associate energy with feelings and the awareness grows between pleasant energy versus unpleasant energy and situations.

As the baby develops into a toddler and young child, the realization creeps in, that what is felt as love, even by the closest people in the child's life, does not always stay the same. The knowledge that this wonderful feeling can dissipate and be replaced with a separate feeling of loss (feeling alone and abandoned) begins to affect how the energy of love is experienced. What was once simply awareness now becomes a craving and desire. The young child who remembers and wants love more than anything else tries to determine what is good and bad and what will bring that attention and love back into its energy field. These feelings adapt into judgments. The child works to create a pattern they can understand and repeat with success. This is achieved by observing and learning what reaction, each action brings. The child wishes to learn which actions create positive attention and which are punished with the withdrawal of love.

This adaptation is created from the fear of loss. From this point, the judging begins. One can observe this activity even in very young children, as a child feels ignored by a parent and acts out in various ways to discover which action will bring attention. This continues into adulthood as we make judgments on the experiences in our lives. For many people, this becomes the path they continue on, without going any further to understand where this is coming from. Perhaps they even derive a certain comfort in judging, as they develop a sense of control that they understand right from wrong and how things should be.

At this point, we empathize that judging comes from fear and a sense of loss. Now we must understand the concept of discernment. Discernment comes from love and a sense of understanding a situation for what it is on a greater scale, without the same type of emotional need and attachment. Judgment confines, Discernment releases. Judgment frightens, Discernment nurtures. Judgment puts people in a box; Discernment frees souls to be, while understanding the greater purpose and the universal laws of action and reaction. With Discernment, also comes wisdom which includes understanding the motive behind the motive. For the sake of this lesson, this wisdom teaching can be described as understanding why a person is doing the action they are doing and what they hope to gain or accomplish from this action.

As the student progresses on their spiritual journey, they become aware of the evolving energy with each experience. With this realization, it becomes clear each day that to judge is very difficult to do as your own life and experiences change quickly. You find that what you judged or understood to be one way a year ago, now may feel completely different to you. You begin to understand that there is not such a concrete right and wrong or black and white. The world is made up of many shades of grey and a thousand other colors and it's based more on perception and where one is at emotionally and mentally at any given moment.

With this understanding, you are discovering that inside of you, there is an essence of Divine Wisdom and Knowledge. Once you have experienced its strength and peace, you begin to bring it into your life so that you become aware of its Conscious, Spiritual Energy. Many people experience their first "knowing" of this Divine Wisdom, by calling it intuition. At this realization, the question then becomes how does one take those occasional flashes of intuition, and turn them into a deeper connection? How do you reach inside of your Soul and connect with the Divine Source and make it effective so that it will not only transform your own life, but also transform the environment around you?

The answer began with facing the fears which were created from past experiences. This understanding develops into the knowledge that those fears became judgments and that now judging can no longer be a part of who you are. This path is walked in a series of steps including being honest with yourself and others at all times. In addition, it means sincerity; telling the truth in daily living, rather than previous well meant manipulations. It means love at all times, no matter what the circumstance or situation. This type of divine love means true unselfishness to the extent and power of your Soul.

As you walk on this journey, you will be rewarded with your Higher Self connecting more directly with you. As a result, you will find less need to judge. What is replaced in this space, is discernment. This is because the Higher Self is able to work with you more frequently, as you are altering your body back towards the pure state of being.

As you enter into the wisdom teachings, the path continues to evolve. The journey from knowledge to wisdom is described in the esoteric teachings as:

The Spiraling Path of Enlightenment

The first step on this journey is experiencing LOVE (pure love, of a higher note, love for all of humanity, love in all things, and love of all people regardless of how it affects you personally).

The second step on the path is TRUTH (To truly be honest with yourself in all cases, and with others, done in the gentlest way possible).

From here, discernment and the resulting wisdom and guidance of the Higher Self, lead the soul to actions of COMPASSION (to be unselfish, to give freely without thought of reciprocation, to give without thought of return, without gaining special favor).

The journey continues from here into PURITY (to cleanse one's thoughts, emotions, mind and heart, and to have the best thoughts for oneself and others, including all of humanity).

There are many other steps from this point of the spiraling path. However, at this point of advancement, discernment is now working with your developing intuition. It serves to give you an enhanced understanding of the world around you including what is being experienced and felt by others. We are only skimming over some of the steps in this process, such as having worked through releasing the emotions and understanding that thoughts are things. Our hope is that the end result can still be understood with this explanation.

As the soul releases old thoughts, emotions and fears, the emotional reaction of judgment is removed and the pearl of wisdom known as discernment grows in its place.

The difference between this energy as a child and the energy you now radiate is that it is coupled with wisdom. In this place, one has discernment, eyes in which to see. This allows the soul to know the motive behind the motive. When you have this ability, you hear what the true intention is behind the words that are said, you see the true intent behind the action and you are aware of what is not being shown on the physical earth plane.

Discernment is an important tool to have on the journey. It is achieved when the need to feed the ego and retain control is released by the mind. Once this occurs, the mind and soul embrace and open to the Divine in faith and love. As you begin to work on this process, do not be discouraged, as it does not happen overnight. It takes time and searching deep within to find the means of dropping the personal self, losing the ego and then rediscovering yourself in a spiritual regeneration and rebirth.

As we mentioned previously, during this process you will discover many parts of yourself which you have pulled apart and hidden, not wanting to deal with those issues from so long ago. The experience of reconnecting with these emotions and thoughts are frightening at first. However, when faced in the light they lead to transformational experiences which are described by many students as life-altering.

It can be done and is referred to as "Embracing the Light." The peace and joy felt inside is indescribable when this occurs. It transforms not only your relationships with others, but also your relationship with yourself, as well as the Divine.

If you feel that this is your time to move from judgment to discernment and you are ready to take this action on your spiritual journey, then begin with this knowledge:

Prayer, in the right form, with conscious thought and intent, can transform an individual and create a regeneration of the self.

Only you will know if the time is right to proceed on this path. If it is not, wait until you feel the strength inside to continue, for this is a journey of great proportions and timing is important. This is your journey. You will receive more than one opportunity to walk the path in this lifetime, so have no fear.

Chapter Eleven

Transforming from Neophyte to Initiate

"The day will come when, after harnessing space, the winds, the tides and gravitation, we shall harness for God the energies of love. And on that day, for the second time in the history of the world, we shall have discovered fire."
-- Tielhard de Chardin --

To begin the transformation from a Neophyte student to an Initiate, the student most undergo a series of tests, some of which are given on the earth plane and others which are presented to the student from teachers on the other planes. These rituals and experiences will not be discussed in this venue, as they are uniquely personal for each student. In addition, the purpose of this book is to share information on what the experience is like to become a Neophyte student of the esoteric teachings.

There are many other lessons and teachings which a Neophyte will be exposed to before they can proceed onward to becoming an Initiate. In their course of study, they will have explored various systems and theories of the uni-verse and multi-verse, pondered the planes of existence, prepared for future astral travels, hypothesized on sacred geometry and principles of science and mathematics and studied ancient teachings of astrology, tarot, runes, crystals and gemstones, and auras and chakras along with the power of music, color and vocal sounds. They have practiced ancient techniques of breathing, wrestled with their egos, faced their mortality and their immortality and explored various paths of religion and spirituality.

Throughout all of these wisdom teachings, it has also become glaringly apparent to them, that what they thought they knew, they did not, and what they do know, is most assuredly the tip of the proverbial iceberg as they journey further.

A Neophyte desiring to become an Initiate must be open to the understanding that what they have learned to date is oft described as the Lesser Mysteries and that the Greater Mysteries have only been touched upon at this point. They understand and accept that they may be asked again to un-learn and explore anew all which was presented to them in the beginning.

To say this journey is for the few, can not even begin to accurately describe the hearty, strong willed people who brave this exploration of heart, mind and soul.

Students are tested on their understanding of the balance between masculine and feminine. They face challenges to determine if they are working to live in love from the heart chakra. There are tests of patience and discernment. Neophyte students think the same lesson is being repeated over and over, while Initiates see the deeper wisdoms revealed in the lesson as they evolve. There are many other tests they face, which are not to be revealed in this book, for the mystical journey waits for those who wish to proceed.

It is worth noting that one can apply to become a Neophyte in the mystery schools, though not all are accepted. However one can not apply to become an Initiate. It is an energy expression which is recognized on this plane and others. The offer is extended to the student after careful consideration and consultation with teachers, light beings and guides on the earth plane and other planes. Those who enter this challenge, find it to be most rewarding and fulfilling.

This concludes our explanation of nine of the life altering lessons which Neophyte students experience in their course of study with the esoteric teachings. If you are wondering if such a journey is right for you, ask yourself these questions:

1. What attracted me to reading this book?

2. How did I feel while reading this book, did it resonate with me on some level?

3. Am I content with my life as it is, or do I have a feeling I am here to do something more than I am currently doing?

4. Do I often have dreams or thoughts about living in other times? Do I connect or have strange feelings when others speak of Egypt, Greece or ancient myths and legends?

5. Is my current spiritual and life path giving me peace and contentment?

6. Do I feel a shift within my self? Is there awareness that it is time for me to awaken, yet I am unsure what that truly means?

7. Have I explored various religious and metaphysical concepts, but found them lacking in some way? Were they unable to answer the questions I had?

If you answered yes to more than three of these questions, than you may wish to further explore the esoteric mystery teachings.

It is our wish that this book will have served to inspire and stimulate your heart, mind and soul and encourage you on your journey. There are schools of enlightenment and teachers who are willing to teach the mysteries to students who are ready in this lifetime.

For those who prefer to read more about the ancient mysteries, there are more books than one would imagine which are easily accessed on both western and eastern mystery teachings and philosophies.

You will find that each teacher has their own way of expressing and teaching these concepts, choosing the path which resonates for them. Each does the work according to how they are guided to do so, by their higher self, their teachers and guides, and the Brotherhood and other beings of light from the other planes. Regardless of the messenger or the path chosen, the universal truths remain just that and can always be identified as such. They continue to be expressed in various forms; however, the end result is always a greater understanding of self and higher consciousness.

The way teachings are presented are also altered according to the times and society. For example, when studying ancient Egyptian mysteries, the focus was on the noble understanding of the rituals and acts, while in ancient Greece we see a greater encouragement of philosophy and discussion to understand the mysteries. Both of which are important to achieve balance within the soul.

All things adapt with the thoughts and energy around them. This includes the parables of the teachings as they seek to teach by using modern day scenarios. The key is to keep an open mind and focus on what each lesson is saying at its core level.

Remember, as we mentioned in the beginning of this book, "Do not believe a word we have said, trust in yourself and follow your heart." "Ask your higher self to be your guide and never forget to ask for your highest and best to always be made manifest through to you and it undoubtedly shall."

In love and light to you on your journey,

Kala

For more information on the mystery school Stella Maris, visit www.templeofstellamaris.org

To listen to interviews with people sharing their knowledge on metaphysical, spiritual and paranormal topics, visit the Explore Your Spirit with Kala Talk Show: www.exploreyourspirit.com

"Your vision will become clear only when you can look into your own heart.
Who looks outside, dreams; who looks inside, awakens."
-- Carl Jung --

About The Author

As a small child, Kala could be found in the library studying and teaching the history of ancient cultures and mythologies from around the world to other children and adults who were willing to listen. Raised by parents and grandparents who encouraged her spiritual exploration and education, (while pregnant with Kala, her mother was given her name in a dream - "Kala Renee", meaning "time reborn"), Kala returned in this lifetime with what her grandparents referred to as "the gift", with psychic ability and prophetic dreams, passed down from her grandfather and great-grandmother of Celtic Scottish and French lineage. In childhood, she began to experience prophetic dreams which she referred to as going to night school. At the age of thirteen Kala was calculating astrological charts by hand along with reading tarot for friends. As she progressed, her psychic abilities and understanding increased and she further connected with the symbols given to her in dreams, along with guides who worked with her from this realm.

Born in Louisiana, she has lived in distinct and powerful earth energy areas including Alaska, Hawaii, Washington, California, and Florida, which enhanced her spiritual growth and understanding of people and the world, as well as allowed her the opportunity to study with a variety of spiritual teachers and philosophers. Kala has explored many forms of spirituality including eastern mysticism, eastern and western esoteric teachings, earth wisdom, and the philosophies and wisdom of ancient cultures. Her journey led her again in this lifetime, to meet under the most mysterious and synchronistic set of circumstances, Egyptian and Greek esoteric teachers who indoctrinated her into the esoteric teachings with lessons and rituals conducted on the earth plane and in the spiritual realms.

A noted Esoteric Teacher, Intuitive, and Metaphysical Talk Show Host, Kala lectures and teaches classes and workshops on a wide variety of ancient esoteric teachings and works with students who wish to explore their lives at the soul level through the esoteric mystery school of Stella Maris. (TempleofStellaMaris.org)

Her Talk Show, "Explore Your Spirit with Kala", (ExploreYourSpirit.com) offers enlightening shows with World Renowned Authors, Artists, Teachers and Researchers delving into Metaphysical, Spiritual and Paranormal Topics as well as New Discoveries in the Scientific and Spiritual Arenas.

In her spare time, Kala conducts paranormal research with The Rowan Society (rowansociety.org) and is working on her next book.

Reality is what you make it

RE reality PRESS

LIFE CHANGING BOOKS AND DVDS BY REALITY PRESS

Printed in the United States
124854LV00002B/134/A

9 781934 588031